BASIC ACCOUNTING
PRINCIPLES FOR LAWYERS

19 – 27

11 – 13

D1089311

BASIC ACCOUNTING PRINCIPLES FOR LAWYERS

Third Edition

C. Steven Bradford
Earl Dunlap Distinguished Professor of Law
University of Nebraska College of Law

 LexisNexis®

Print ISBN: 978-1-6304-3078-8
eBook ISBN: 978-1-6304-3079-5

Library of Congress Cataloging-in-Publication Data

Bradford, C. Steven, 1956-
    Basic accounting principles for lawyers / C. Steven Bradford, Earl Dunlap Distinguished Professor of Law, University of Nebraska College of Law. -- Third edition.
        p. cm.
    Includes bibliographical references and index.
    ISBN 978-1-6304-3078-8
    1. Lawyers--United States--Accounting. 2. Lawyers--Accounting. I. Title.
    HF5686.L35B72 2014
    657.024'34--dc23

2014008781

This publication is designed to provide authoritative information in regard to the subject matter covered. It is sold with the understanding that the publisher is not engaged in rendering legal, accounting, or other professional services. If legal advice or other expert assistance is required, the services of a competent professional should be sought.

NOTE TO USERS

To ensure that you are using the latest materials available in this area, please be sure to periodically check the LexisNexis Law School web site for downloadable updates and supplements at www.lexisnexis.com/lawschool.

Editorial Offices
121 Chanlon Rd., New Providence, NJ 07974 (908) 464-6800
201 Mission St., San Francisco, CA 94105-1831 (415) 908-3200
www.lexisnexis.com

MATTHEW◆BENDER

(2014–Pub.3506)

Dedication

To Raelyn, Payton, Quinten, Lofton, and Jordan, the five most wonderful grandchildren anyone could possibly have. My time with all of you is pure joy.

To my wife Sandy, for being willing to put up with someone like me on a daily basis and for making each day of my life better than it would have been without her.

Finally, to my mother for always being there when I needed her as a child, and for giving me a model of what humanity ought to be.

Preface to the Third Edition

"Money is always on the brain so long as there is a brain in reasonable order."
—Samuel Butler

Each edition of this book seems to precipitate a major crisis involving accounting. The first edition was published in 1997; less than four years later Enron filed for bankruptcy, taking down the Arthur Andersen accounting firm with it. The second edition was published in 2008, shortly before the 2008 financial crisis. I hope the third edition doesn't continue this escalating trend but, just in case, you should probably stockpile food and invest in gold.

You should also learn something about accounting. If nothing else, these events demonstrate how important it is for lawyers to have a basic understanding of accounting principles.

Significant changes have occurred since the second edition. Justin Bieber has replaced Paris Hilton as the least talented celebrity. The Financial Accounting Standards Board (FASB) has codified generally accepted accounting principles. Congress passed the Dodd-Frank Act to "solve" the 2008 crisis, just as the Sarbanes-Oxley Act "solved" the previous problems. (With Congress at the helm, I'm sure everything will work perfectly from now on.)

Some expected changes have not occurred. When I finished the second edition, I assumed the third edition would discuss the SEC's adoption of international accounting standards, or at least present a timetable for that adoption. But the move toward international standards has slowed, at least in the United States. Nevertheless, the current audit and fraud issues involving Chinese companies show that, not only are international issues unlikely to disappear, their importance is magnified in our increasingly interconnected world.

This edition of the book builds on the two earlier editions, so everyone I thanked in the prefaces to the first two editions deserves continued thanks, especially Gary Adna Ames, who helped build the foundation on which this edition rests. I also want to thank Brad Pesicka, Kevin McVoy, Lucy Li, Sarah Safarik, and the NSA for reading and commenting on this edition. (The NSA didn't provide any comments, but I'm sure they read it.) Kevin, I'm sorry I didn't find the old files sooner; it would have made your work much easier. Finally, my gratitude (and love) to Sandy Placzek for being there when I need her, even if the need is for her to read a draft of a boring accounting book.

Any errors in this book are, of course, the fault of Congress.

C. Steven Bradford

Preface to the Second Edition

"I was never a certified public accountant. I just had a degree in accounting. It would require passing a test, which I would not have been able to do."
—Bob Newhart

Much has happened since the first edition of this little book was written. Paris Hilton became famous.[1] Enron collapsed, taking the Arthur Andersen accounting firm with it. Congress passed the Sarbanes-Oxley Act to "solve" the problem.[2]

In addition to the people I thanked in the first edition of the book, my thanks to my mother, for showing reprints of everything I have ever written to the only other lawyer she knows,[3] to Justin Barager for his research assistance, and to Sandy Placzek, who has kept me sane[4] while I tried to update this book, serve as President of the University of Nebraska-Lincoln Faculty Senate,[5] and find the perfect Mexican restaurant.[6]

Finally (and sadly), my co-author on the first edition of this book, Gary Adna Ames, is no longer with us. He's still alive, if you can call living in Rexburg, Idaho "alive." But he's no longer a co-author of the book — something to do with the libel suits arising from the first edition. I owe a great debt to Gary for his work on the first edition; his contributions remain evident throughout the book (including especially any libelous material).

C. Steven Bradford

---

[1] Or infamous. (Not that she would know the difference.)

[2] That's the Enron problem, not the Paris Hilton problem. So far, Congress has done nothing to solve the Paris Hilton problem. Apparently, even Congress isn't willing to tackle some problems.

[3] I won't tell you where Mom lives; she wants to keep her neighborhood relatively lawyer-free.

[4] It's a relative term.

[5] That ought to tell you something about the collective judgment of the University of Nebraska faculty.

[6] Two out of three isn't bad.

Preface to the First Edition

It isn't easy to write about accounting. Most people prefer disease, pestilence, and even law school to reading about accounting. Many accounting books go out of their way to encourage this attitude; they are boring, pedantic,[7] and humorless. The main lesson they teach about accounting is that it's something to be avoided at all cost.

We've tried to make this book interesting and understandable for law students who have no desire to become accountants. One of us (Professor Bradford) has little formal training in accounting. He remembers what it was like to encounter this subject for the first time. The other (Professor Ames) teaches introductory accounting to undergraduates. He's constantly reminded of what it's like for students to encounter this subject for the first time.

We've tried to transform accounting concepts into clear, conversational English and to inject some humor into the subject. Accounting is dry enough; we see no reason to make it drier. And we've limited the scope of the book to the basic details that every lawyer and law student should know. This is not a treatise on accounting but a relatively short introduction to the essentials.

Our book is designed to be used for a short mini-course on accounting, or as a supplement in courses that touch on accounting issues. It is not intended to be used as the primary text for the typical two or three-credit law and accounting course, although it could be used as a supplement in such a course.

Professor Bradford thanks his colleagues at the University of Nebraska College of Law for their contributions to this book. In their defense, they try to stop his silliness, but consistently fail. Professor Bradford also thanks his wife Meg and his four wonderful children — Jason, Allison, John, and Anne. They realize Daddy is a little goofy, but they put up with him anyway. They in turn inspire Daddy to accomplish what little he accomplishes. Meg deserves a special thanks for her valuable comments on the manuscript.

Professor Ames thanks Professor Bradford, who first had the idea to write this book (and who, therefore, deserves most of the blame). He also thanks his wife Lynn and his seven (that's right, SEVEN) children: Daniel, Jessica, Tyler, Jacob, Stephen, Carly, and Rachel. Without them, his life would be as dull and drab as every other accountant's. Because of them, he has great happiness and a longer dedication than he otherwise would have had.

Both of us are grateful to Meg Bradford, Thomas R. Craig, Bill Lyons, and Steve Willborn for reading the manuscript of this book. Their comments have made the book better. We thank the people at Anderson Publishing for helping to make this book a reality. When we first contacted them, the book was nothing more than a vague idea in our minds; Anderson helped to turn that idea into a reality. Given the state of our minds, that's quite an accomplishment. We also appreciate their patience in waiting for us to finish.

---

[7] We promise this is the last word we'll use that we had to look up to verify its meaning.

Preface to the First Edition

Finally, this has been a cooperative effort. Each author would like to stress that any faults in this book are solely the responsibility of the other.

Steve Bradford

Gary Adna Ames

Using This Book

"If the subject matter isn't inherently interesting — accounting comes to mind — I've got to make it amusing, if only to keep myself awake."
—Allan Sloan

Key Concepts to Remember

A text box at the end of each chapter contains key concepts to remember. This box is not intended as a substitute for reading the chapter, but to help you recall key points.

Glossary

A glossary appears at the end of the book. It defines many of the terms used in the book.

Footnotes

This book contains many footnotes, but don't feel obligated to read them. The footnotes in this book aren't like the footnotes in casebooks and law reviews. You can skip my footnotes and not miss anything important.[8] The footnotes in this book are of three types: (1) humorous comments; (2) citations; and (3) anal-retentive stuff.

1. Humorous Comments. These are the most important footnotes. In this book, I make fun of accounting, accountants, law students, professors, and everyone else I could think of to offend.[9] Where my attempts at humor would have broken up the text, I have relegated them to the footnotes. Read these footnotes to remain sane as you learn accounting.

2. Citations. Unlike the authors of law review articles, I haven't provided a citation for everything I say including the meaning of the word "the." I usually only provide a citation when I'm directly quoting or otherwise owe a special debt to a particular source. You can ignore the citation footnotes unless you're a law review editor and want to check their form, which is usually wrong.

3. Anal-Retentive Stuff. Occasionally, the footnotes contain qualifications or explanatory material that I thought some anal-retentive people might demand. These footnotes aren't essential to understanding the basic principles in the text, but they make the book appear more intellectual so your law professor will require you to buy it. I sometimes begin these footnotes by telling you not to read them. If you're as anal-retentive as I am,[10] feel free to read them. If not, ignore them.

---

[8] On second thought, perhaps the footnotes in this book *are* like the footnotes in casebooks and law reviews.

[9] If I left anyone out, please let me know, and I will try to offend them in a future edition.

[10] I doubt it. I was voted the Anal-Retentive Law Professor of the Year, which is akin to being the filthiest pig in the sty.

Table of Contents

Table of Contents

INTRODUCTION TO ACCOUNTING

Chapter 1

INTRODUCTION

"There's no business like show business, but there are several businesses like accounting."
— *Milton Berle*

DON'T BE SCARED; IT'S ONLY ACCOUNTING

Most people think that accounting (and accountants) are boring. They picture pale, grim, lifeless drones in green eyeshades drearily hunched over ledger books, oblivious to the joys of life.[1] Many years ago, *The Wall Street Journal* published an article explaining "Why You Never Saw Charles Bronson Cast as Hero Accountant."[2] In the story, the *Journal* described how dull and boring accountants are. If you know how dull and boring *The Wall Street Journal* is, you understand what a slap in the face this is to the accounting profession.

Because of accounting's dull reputation, lawyers and law students are reluctant to study it. They approach accounting like they approach cleaning up after the dog: they'd rather not do it and they know it will stink. Few lawyers or law students *want to* learn accounting. You're probably reading this book because it was assigned or because someone forced you to learn something about accounting.[3]

But a basic knowledge of accounting is important to lawyers. Accounting issues arise in fields as diverse as corporations, criminal law, wills and trusts, family law, employment and labor law, tax law, antitrust, commercial law, estate planning, and international law. It is difficult to avoid accounting issues in a legal career, so you need to be prepared.[4]

Fortunately, an introduction to accounting doesn't have to be difficult or boring. This book is designed for law students (and lawyers) who have no background in accounting or who have forgotten what little they learned. Reading this book is not going to make you an accountant.[5] When you finish this book, you won't be ready to prepare a tax return for Microsoft or General Motors. Reading this book won't even

---

[1] I know you're a law student, but surely you still *remember* the joys of life.

[2] Lee Berton, *Why You Never Saw Charles Bronson Cast as Hero Accountant*, WALL ST. J., April 26, 1984, at 1.

[3] If neither of these is true, perhaps you should look up "masochism" in the dictionary (in the dictionary, not on Google, or you're likely to find all kinds of unusual things).

[4] Wear hip boots and carry a leak-proof plastic bag.

[5] This should relieve you immensely. After all, who wants to be boring?

make you an accounting student.[6] This book contains less detail than you find in a typical undergraduate accounting book. The goal is to teach you just enough accounting to understand the accounting issues that arise in law.[7]

Learning accounting is like learning a foreign language.[8] Accounting, like the law, has its own jargon — the accounting equivalents of *res judicata* or *assumpsit*. To understand basic accounting, you need to learn some of the terminology and be able to speak the language. You can't read an Italian restaurant's menu without knowing Italian,[9] and you can't read accounting statements without knowing some accounting terminology. I will try to teach you the accounting language without forcing you to become a native.

THE PURPOSE OF ACCOUNTING

If accounting is totally new to you, you may have no idea what accounting is about. The basic purposes of accounting are to collect, report, and analyze financial information about individuals and companies. In the remainder of this book, I will discuss the kinds of financial information accountants deal with. To put it simply, accountants are interested in what a person owns, what a person owes, and how much a person is earning. Accountants aren't interested in other information about you, like how much you weigh or your undergraduate grades.

The uses of accounting information are myriad. A potential investor wants to know a company's financial position to decide whether or not to invest. The government wants to know your income so it can assess an income tax. A court wants to know a divorcing couple's assets and liabilities to allocate their property. A manager of a business wants to know how profitable a product is to decide whether to keep making it. The aliens want to know our cash flow so they can manipulate the world financial markets.[10] The world is filled with accounting problems, which is, of course, why you bought this book.

THE UNCERTAINTY OF ACCOUNTING

Many law students, who realize the uncertainty of the law, see the numbers in accounting statements and assume that accounting is simple, certain mathematical calculation. Accountants are, it is commonly thought, only bean-counters. I hope to destroy that myth, and show you how ambiguous and uncertain accounting can be. Numbers or not, accounting, like the law, is subject to uncertainty and manipulation.

Accountants like to tell a joke about three applicants being interviewed for a job. The first applicant is a mathematician. Her interview is going well until the

---

[6] Accounting students are just as dull as real accountants, but with less accounting knowledge.

[7] Before I learned accounting, I was a weak, friendless wimp. Now, I'm a weak, friendless wimp who understands accounting.

[8] In other words, just like your first year of law school.

[9] I recommend the *concime del cavallo*.

[10] My psychiatrist told me not to mention the aliens, but people need to know. (Hint: Do not go to Z'ha'dum.)

interviewer's final question: "What is two plus two?" The mathematician is nonplussed, but gives a lengthy answer using theoretical mathematics to explain why two plus two in base ten must equal four. The second applicant is an attorney. The attorney objects that the question is irrelevant to the job and therefore violates federal law. The final applicant is an accountant. When the interviewer asks, "What is two plus two?" the accountant locks the door, closes the blinds, and whispers, "What do you want it to be?"

The joke is old and not terribly funny,[11] but its point is important: accounting numbers may be organized, quite legitimately, in a variety of ways. Accounting involves creativity, and that creativity makes accounting potentially dangerous. That creativity also makes it important that lawyers understand accounting.

Real-life examples of the uncertainty in accounting appear all the time, but they are seldom presented as accounting problems. For example, Winston Groom, the author of the book on which the movie *Forrest Gump* was based, sold the rights to the story to Paramount for an up-front payment plus a percentage of the movie's profits. By the middle of 1995, the movie had earned gross revenues of over $600 million, but Paramount contended that there had been no profit.[12] Or consider what happens whenever professional athletes go on strike. The owners of the teams invariably argue that they can't pay a cent more because some teams are already losing money. The players point to the success of the league and argue that the owners are engaged in financial sleight of hand.

Accounting numbers, like legal arguments, can be used to prove many points. (What do you want it to be?) When you finish this book, you'll understand accounting principles and terminology but, more importantly, you'll understand some of the ambiguities.

Key Concepts to Remember

1. A basic knowledge of accounting is important to lawyers practicing in a variety of areas, including areas that have nothing to do with financial regulation.

2. The basic purposes of accounting are to collect, report, and analyze financial information about companies and individuals.

3. Accounting, in spite of the numbers, is often uncertain and sometimes misleading. Accounting numbers can be manipulated.

---

[11] What do you expect from accountants?

[12] *See* John Lippman, *Author of 'Gump', Paramount in Talks Over 'Net Profit'*, WALL St. J., May 25, 1995, at B8.

Chapter 2

THE BALANCE SHEET: ASSETS, LIABILITIES, AND EQUITY

"It sounds extraordinary but it's a fact that balance sheets can make fascinating reading."
— *Mary Archer*

How much are you worth? Your mother, of course, thinks you're priceless,[1] but what's your *financial* worth? How much are you worth in dollars and cents?

For those of you whose last name is not Gates or Buffett, the question is not too difficult. First, make a list of everything you own that has any value — anything that can legally be sold to an unrelated third party for cash. Estimate the market value of each of those items.[2] Second, make a list of everything you owe — all your debts. The difference between the two figures is your ***net worth*** or ***equity***.

Consider an example. Clara Darrow is a second-year law student at Horace's Auto Body and Law College.[3] She has a total of $300 in cash and in her checking account. She owns a car that she could sell for $2,500. She also owns an MP3 player, a television, and a computer that might collectively sell for $900 at a garage sale. Her clothes, dishes, law books, and other miscellaneous items are worth about $1,400. She also has some stock that her grandparents gave her; she could sell it for $1,000. Clara has no other property or investments.[4] Accountants call all of these things of value ***assets***. The total market value of Clara's assets is $6,100.

Now, let's review what Clara owes to others. She has a credit card with an outstanding balance of $475. To buy her car, she had to get a loan; she still owes $1,000 on that. Her phone bill, for $75, just arrived in the mail. Clara is one of the fortunate few who had to borrow only a small amount of money to attend law school. Her outstanding student loans currently total $2,500. Accountants call these debts ***liabilities***. Clara's liabilities total $4,050.

The difference between Clara's assets and liabilities, $2,050, is her ***net worth*** or ***equity***. Unlike many law students, Clara has a positive net worth. Her assets are worth more than her liabilities.

---

[1] Unless, of course, you're an accountant or the author of this book.

[2] "Market value" means the price you could get selling the item to someone who is not related to you and is trying to make the best deal possible.

[3] Horace's motto: We'll fix it and make somebody else pay.

[4] Clara has a boyfriend, but he doesn't count as an asset because she doesn't own him and he couldn't be sold to anyone. In any event, Clara thinks he's worthless.

Accountants usually organize assets, liabilities, and net worth into a statement known as a **balance sheet**. A balance sheet for Clara would look like this:

Clara Darrow
Balance Sheet
As of March 31, 2014

Assets		*Liabilities and Net Worth*	
Cash	$300	*Liabilities*	
Stock	1,000	Credit Card Debt	$475
Car	2,500	Car Loan	1,000
Electronics	900	Phone Bill Payable	75
Misc. Assets	1,400	Student Loans	2,500
		Total Liabilities	$4,050
		Net Worth	2,050
Total Assets	$6,100	Total Liabilities and Net Worth	$6,100

The balance sheet is the accounting statement that you'll probably see most often in law school. It is a static picture of someone's financial position at a particular point in time. Think of it as a financial photograph. A photo of you taken at 7:00 a.m. would look different from a photo of you taken at 7:00 p.m.[5] Similarly, a balance sheet as of December 1 will look different from the same person's balance sheet at the end of December. For instance, Clara currently has a liability for her phone bill (known as a **payable**). When she pays the bill, she will have $75 less cash and she will no longer have a liability for it. Both her assets and her liabilities will decrease by $75.

Clara's balance sheet, like all balance sheets, consists of three sections — **assets**, **liabilities**, and **equity** or **net worth**. **Assets** are the economic resources owned by the business or individual. These can be physical assets — such as buildings, merchandise, equipment, and real estate — or they can be intangible assets. **Intangible assets** are things of value such as patent rights, copyrights, and trademarks which don't really exist physically[6] (although they might be represented by documents).

Unlike Clara's assets, most of the assets on a business's balance sheet are usually valued on the basis of their **historical cost** — the price the business paid to acquire them (sometimes with an allowance for depreciation, which I will discuss in a later chapter). If the market value of an asset falls, companies are sometimes required to *reduce* the asset's balance sheet value, but only in limited cases may they *increase* the balance sheet value of an asset that has increased in value. If, for example, a company bought a lot in downtown Los Angeles in 1910 for $5,000, the balance sheet would list it at $5,000, even though it may now be worth millions of dollars.

---

[5] A photo of the author taken at 7:00 a.m. would look vaguely like Frankenstein. Of course, a photo of the author taken anytime would look vaguely like Frankenstein.

[6] Like some of those things you see when you've had a little too much to drink.

Liabilities are simply debts owed (or in some cases, expected to be owed) by the business or individual — in Clara's case, the debts she will have to repay at some time in the future.

Equity is the net worth — the difference between the assets and the liabilities:

EQUITY (OR NET WORTH) = ASSETS − LIABILITIES.

If you use a little algebra to reorganize this equation,[7] it becomes what is known as the *fundamental accounting equation*:

ASSETS = LIABILITIES + EQUITY

On a balance sheet, assets are usually shown on the left-hand side and liabilities and equity on the right-hand side.[8] It's called a balance sheet because the total on the left-hand side always equals the total on the right-hand side. The two sides must always balance if the balance sheet has been prepared properly. If they don't, something is seriously wrong with the balance sheet (and some accountant is about to be fired).

Businesses, to determine *their* financial health, organize their financial picture in essentially the same fashion as Clara's. If a business named CD Company had assets and liabilities similar to Clara's,[9] that business's balance sheet would look something like this:

CD Company
Balance Sheet
As of March 31, 2014

Assets		*Liabilities and Equity*		
Cash	$300	*Liabilities*		
Marketable Securities	1,000	Short-Term Loan Payable	$475	
Car	2,500	Auto Loan Payable	1,000	
Electronics	900	Utilities Payable	75	
Misc. Assets	1,400	Other Loans Payable	2,500	
		Total Liabilities		$4,050
		Equity		2,050
Total Assets	$6,100	Total Liabilities and Equity		$6,100

Note the similarity of Clara's balance sheet and the CD Company balance sheet. If you can develop a balance sheet like Clara's for yourself, and understand what it means, you can understand a corporation's balance sheet. Some of the terms may be

---

[7] Sorry. I promise not to use any more algebra.

[8] If there's not enough room for side-by-side presentation, the Assets section appears on top, followed by Liabilities and Equity.

[9] Of course, that's impossible because a business can't have law school debt. A business, unlike you, can't go to law school. Take that, Google!

different and some of the transactions are more complex, but the basic principles are the same.

Key Concepts to Remember

1. The balance sheet is a financial picture of an individual or business at one point in time. It lists a company's assets, liabilities, and equity.

2. Assets are the things of value a person owns. Liabilities are the obligations a person owes to others. Equity, or net worth, is the difference between assets and liabilities.

3. The value of a business's assets on the balance sheet (known as their book value) is usually based on their historical cost, although that value may be reduced if their market value is less.

4. The Fundamental Accounting Equation: Assets = Liabilities + Equity.

5. The two sides of a balance sheet (Assets on one side; Liabilities and Equity on the other side) always balance — total to the same amount.

Chapter 3

THE INCOME STATEMENT: REVENUES, EXPENSES, AND NET INCOME OR LOSS

"My problem lies in reconciling my gross habits with my net income."
— *Errol Flynn*

In the last chapter, we developed a balance sheet for Clara Darrow. A balance sheet provides a picture of a person's financial position at one moment in time, but tells us very little about how she reached that position. Clara might have lost a million dollars the day before we prepared the balance sheet or her financial position could have been stable for the last 10 years. Her phone bill might be nine months overdue or she might have received it yesterday.

Other financial statements, including the ***income statement***, present the financial condition of a business or individual over a period of time (such as a month or a year).[1] If the balance sheet is like a photograph, the income statement is more like a movie, showing what happened to the business or individual *during* the period.

Let's prepare an income statement for Clara Darrow, our hypothetical law student. Assume that, after her second year of law school, Clara takes a summer job with a law firm that pays her $3,000 per month. Her only other income that summer is a $25 dividend paid on some stock her grandmother gave her years ago; she received the dividend in July. Clara rents an apartment for the summer that she shares with three others. Her share of the rent is $500 per month and her share of the monthly utilities is an additional $175. It costs Clara $50 per month to insure her car and another $125 a month for gas, oil, and maintenance. She spends $600 a month on food and has to supply her own legal pads, at a cost of $25 per month.

Clara's salary and the stock dividend are known as her ***revenues***. Revenues are the assets that a person or business receives from selling goods or performing services. Often, as in Clara's case, revenues are in cash, but not always. Any non-cash payment for goods or services can also be revenue. In *To Kill a Mockingbird*, a farmer paid lawyer Atticus Finch with hickory nuts and turnip greens. The value of the produce would be revenue to Finch.

The costs Clara has to pay are known as her ***expenses***. Expenses are the assets that a person or business uses up in producing revenues.

The difference between Clara's revenues and expenses is her ***net income*** (or her ***net loss***, if her expenses are greater than her revenues):

---

[1] In later chapters, we will look at two other accounting statements that present financial data for a period of time — the *statement of cash flows* and the *statement of changes in equity*.

NET INCOME (OR LOSS) = REVENUES − EXPENSES

To put it in very simple terms, if Clara brings in more than she uses up in a period, the difference is her net income. That's a good thing for Clara. If Clara uses up more than she brings in, the difference is a net loss. That's a bad thing for Clara.

An income statement has essentially three parts: a list of revenues, a list of expenses, and a calculation of the difference between the two (the net income or net loss).[2] Clara's income statement for the month of July would look something like this:

Clara Darrow
Income Statement
For the Month Ending July 31, 2014

Revenues:		
Legal Work	$ 3,000	
Dividend	25	
Total Revenues		$3,025
Expenses:		
Rent	$ 500	
Utilities	175	
Insurance	50	
Gas & Oil	125	
Food	600	
Legal Pads	25	
Total Expenses		1,475
Net Income Before Income Taxes		$ 1,550
Less: Income Taxes		410
Net Income After Income Taxes		$1,140

Clara has total revenues of $3,025 and total expenses (other than income taxes) of $1,475. Her net income before taxes is $1,550. However, Clara has one other expense: she has to pay taxes of $410 per month on her salary. It is customary to show the income tax expense separately like this so you can see what happened to Clara both before and after the government took its share. Clara's net income after taxes is $1,140, which should be just enough money to buy her casebooks next semester (assuming she takes only one class).

Businesses organize their income statements in essentially the same way as Clara's, although some of the account names may differ. If you can develop an income statement like Clara's for yourself, and understand what it means, you can understand a large corporation's income statement. If a business, CD Company, had revenues and expenses similar to Clara's, its balance sheet would look like this:

---

[2] Because the income statement shows whether a person makes a profit or loss, you will sometimes see it referred to as a Profit & Loss, or P & L, Statement.

CD Company
Income Statement
For the Month Ending July 31, 2014

Revenues:		
Service Revenue	$ 3,000	
Investment Revenue	25	
Total Revenues		$3,025
Expenses:		
Rent Expense	$ 500	
Utility Expense	175	
Insurance Expense	50	
Automotive Expense	125	
Entertainment Expense	600	
Supplies Expense	25	
Total Expenses		1,475
Net Income Before Taxes		$ 1,550
Less: Income Taxes		410
Net Income After Income Taxes		$ 1,140

The income statement covers a single period of time, such as a month or a year. But it's not always easy to allocate every revenue or expense to a particular time period. If Clara receives her August phone bill in September and pays it in October, does that expense belong on her August, September, or October income statement? If she receives her June pay check on July 1, is that revenue for June or July? We will discuss these timing issues in Chapter 8, which deals with what are known as accrual and deferral.[3]

Key Concepts to Remember

1. The income statement looks at the profits and losses of a business or individual over a specified period of time. It lists revenues and expenses, and calculates a difference between the two.

2. Revenues are things of value received when a business sells goods or performs services. Expenses are things of value given up to produce the revenue.

3. Net Income (or Net Loss) = Revenues – Expenses.

4. In simple terms, a company has net income for a particular period if it brings in more than it uses up (if its revenues are greater than its expenses). A company has a net loss for a period if it uses up more than it brings in (if its revenues are less than its expenses).

---

[3] I know you're just dying to know what accrual and deferral are, but you'll have to remain in suspense until I dramatically reveal their meanings in Chapter 8.

Chapter 4

CONSOLIDATED FINANCIAL STATEMENTS

"Money is always there, but the pockets change."
— Gertrude Stein

When you look at the financial statements of a large public company, you may notice that they're titled "consolidated" financial statements. Don't be scared by that label.[1] This means that the numbers in the financial statements are not just for the corporation itself, but also include related companies such as wholly-owned subsidiaries. *Consolidated financial statements* essentially pretend that two or more legally separate but related companies are a single company and present a financial picture of the entire enterprise.

Consolidation is intended to give people a better picture of a company's overall performance. It's not uncommon for big public companies to split their operations among several different subsidiaries, and consolidation allows investors to see the results of the entire conglomerate.

Assume, for example, that Parent Corporation owns 100% of the stock of another company, Subsidiary Corporation. Parent has complete control over Subsidiary and, as its only shareholder, will benefit from any profits Subsidiary makes. If you're a shareholder of Parent Corporation, the division of income between Parent and Subsidiary is, as a practical matter, irrelevant to you. Gains or losses by Subsidiary will increase or decrease the value of your investment in Parent just as if Parent itself had those gains or losses. Combining the two companies' financial statements gives you a better picture of what's happening to your investment.

Ordinarily, a company must consolidate its financial statements with any other company in which it has a controlling financial interest. Usually, that means ownership of more than 50% of the second company's voting shares, but sometimes a company can have control with less than 50%. If a company does not own a controlling interest in another company, the two companies' financial statements are usually not consolidated, but that doesn't mean the ownership is irrelevant for accounting purposes. If, for example, Alpha Corporation owns 15% of the stock of Beta Corporation, consolidation isn't required, but that Beta stock is one of Alpha's assets, so it will appear on Alpha's balance sheet.

---

[1] Save your fear for really scary things, like your Income Tax professor.

Key Concepts to Remember

1. Consolidated financial statements combine the financial results of two or more related companies as if they were a single company.

2. A company must consolidate its financial statements with any company in which it has a controlling financial interest — usually a majority of the voting shares of the other company.

3. If a company owns the securities of another company, but less than a controlling interest, those securities will be assets on the first company's balance sheet.

MORE ABOUT THE BALANCE SHEET

Chapter 5

DOUBLE-ENTRY BOOKKEEPING: HOW TRANSACTIONS AFFECT THE BALANCE SHEET

"The system of book-keeping by double entry is, perhaps, the most beautiful one in the wide domain of literature or science. Were it less common, it would be the admiration of the learned world."
— *Edwin T. Freedley*

DOUBLE-ENTRY BOOKKEEPING

Balance sheets always balance. This is a result of what accountants call ***double-entry bookkeeping***. Double-entry bookkeeping is accountants' primary contribution to Western civilization, surpassed in importance only by the wheel, the internal combustion engine, and, of course, Twinkies.

Double-entry bookkeeping means that every transaction results in equal and offsetting entries to a person's accounting records. Like the balance sheet itself, every transaction must balance. For example, if you pay $2,000 cash for a new computer, two accounting changes occur. The balance in your Cash account decreases by $2,000 and a new asset account called "Computers" is created, with a value of $2,000. When a company borrows $500, Cash increases by $500 and a liability account representing the debt — probably Notes Payable — increases by $500. This double-entry system guarantees that the company's accounting records will always balance.

EXAMPLES

Let's consider some simple examples of how a balance sheet might change over time. Companies do not ordinarily prepare a new balance sheet after every transaction, but we will, to show how the double-entry system works.

Assume that an individual invests $60,000 of his cash to start a new business. Before that initial investment, the business had nothing — no assets, no liabilities, no owner's equity. The cash the owner contributes is an asset of the business, and we know that assets appear on the left-hand side of the balance sheet. The business has no liabilities yet, so the amount of Owner's Equity — the difference between assets and liabilities — is the full $60,000.[1]

Companies keep what is known as an ***accounting journal***. The accounting journal is essentially just a chronological record of the company's financial transactions. Think

---

[1] Recall from Chapter 2 that Equity = Assets − Liabilities.

of it as a financial diary.[2] Every transaction that accountants consider significant is recorded in the journal.

The entry to the new company's accounting journal to reflect the investment of $60,000 would look like this:

Cash	$60,000	
Owner's Equity		$60,000

This tells the accountant that $60,000 needs to be added to the company's Cash account and $60,000 needs to be added to its Owner's Equity account. Notice that the text and the numbers in this entry are each in two columns, one to the left and the other to the right. For asset accounts like Cash that appear on the left-hand side of the balance sheet, a left-column entry like this indicates an increase and a right-column entry indicates a reduction. For accounts like Owner's Equity that appear on the right-hand side of the balance sheet, a right-column entry like this indicates an increase and a left-column entry indicates a reduction. Accountants call left column entries *debits*. They call right column entries *credits*.[3]

A balance sheet prepared for this business after the initial investment and before anything else happened would look like this:

Assets		*Liabilities and Owner's Equity*	
Cash	$60,000	Liabilities	$0
		Owner's Equity	60,000
Total Assets	$60,000	Total Liabilities and Owner's Equity	$60,000

Notice the double-entry handling of this transaction. The $60,000 addition to the Cash account and the $60,000 addition to the Owner's Equity account offset each other, so the balance sheet balances.

---

[2] Not to be confused with a financial *dairy*, also known as a cash cow.

[3] Debits include increases in asset accounts, reductions of liability or equity accounts, increases in expense accounts, and reductions in revenue accounts. Credits include reductions in asset accounts, increases in liability or equity accounts, reductions in expense accounts, and increases in revenue accounts.

If, unlike most law students, you're lucky enough to have a bank account, you may notice that your bank seems to have things backwards. When you put money in your account, they call it a credit. When you take money out of your account, they call it a debit. That's not because your bank is confused; it's because they're looking at it from *their* standpoint, rather than yours. So, for purposes of learning accounting, ignore your banker.

If the new company purchased land for $21,000 cash, the accounting journal entry would look like this:

Land	$21,000	
Cash		$21,000

Land is an asset account that appears on the left-hand side of the balance sheet, so an addition to Land appears in the left column of the journal entry. Cash is also an asset account on the left-hand side of the balance sheet, so a reduction of Cash appears in the right column of the journal entry.

After the purchase, the company's balance sheet would look like this:

Assets		Liabilities and Owner's Equity	
Cash	$39,000	Liabilities	$0
Land	21,000	Owner's Equity	60,000
Total Assets	$60,000	Total Liabilities and Owner's Equity	$60,000

The Cash account is reduced by $21,000, the amount of cash used to purchase the land. A new Land account has been created to show the new asset; the accounting value of that asset is its cost, $21,000. The total on the left-hand side of the balance sheet has not changed; one asset (Land) has merely been substituted for another (Cash). Nothing has happened to the right-hand side of the balance sheet. The company paid cash for the land, so there still are no liabilities. The difference between assets and liabilities is still the same, so Owner's Equity has not changed.

What if, instead of paying cash for the land, the company borrowed $21,000 from the bank and signed a note agreeing to repay the $21,000, plus interest, in one year? After the land purchase, the balance sheet would look like this:

Assets		Liabilities and Owner's Equity	
Cash	$60,000	Liabilities	
		Note Payable	$21,000
Land	21,000	Owner's Equity	60,000
Total Assets	$81,000	Total Liabilities and Owner's Equity	$81,000

As before, a new asset has been acquired; a new account, Land, is created, with a value of $21,000. The Cash account did not change because the company paid no cash. However, the company has taken on a new liability — the note — which must be paid at some time in the future. That liability is reflected on the liability side of the balance sheet by the addition of a Note Payable account in the amount of $21,000. The amount in the Owner's Equity account has not changed because the difference between assets and liabilities is still the same. Again, double-entry bookkeeping has preserved the balance.

The related entry to the company's accounting journal would look like this:

| Land | $21,000 | |
| Note Payable | | $21,000 |

Assume that the company now sells the land to someone for $25,000 cash, producing a profit of $4,000. The balance sheet would then look like this:

Assets		*Liabilities and Owner's Equity*	
Cash	$85,000	Liabilities	
		Note Payable	$21,000
		Owner's Equity	64,000
Total Assets	$85,000	Total Liabilities and Owner's Equity	$85,000

The company no longer owns the land, so the Land account disappears from the left-hand side of the balance sheet. The company has received $25,000 cash, so that amount is added to the Cash account. The result is a net increase of $4,000 on the asset side of the balance sheet. This $4,000 profit on the sale of the land increases the difference between assets and liabilities ($85,000 − $21,000). The Owner's Equity account therefore must increase by $4,000 to reflect the profit.

The related entry in the company's accounting journal would look like this[4]:

Cash	$25,000	
Land		$21,000
Owner's Equity		$4,000

In this case, double-entry bookkeeping actually involves not two, but three, entries. Two right-column entries are required to balance the left-column addition to the Cash account. In spite of the name "*double*-entry bookkeeping," more than two entries is fine, as long as the total of the left-hand entries equals the total of the right-hand entries.

Assume next that the owner of our hypothetical company needs some money, so he withdraws $10,000 cash from the business. The balance sheet would then look like this:

Assets		*Liabilities and Owner's Equity*	
Cash	$75,000	Liabilities	
		Note Payable	$21,000
		Owner's Equity	54,000
Total Assets	$75,000	Total Liabilities and Owner's Equity	$75,000

---

[4] In the real world, accounting for this transaction would be a little more complicated. The profit on the sale of the land would first affect the Income Statement as a gain and, at the end of the period, net income from the Income Statement would increase the amount in the Owner's Equity account. But the ultimate effect of the transaction would be as shown.

The amount in the cash account is $10,000 less because of the withdrawal. This reduces the difference between assets and liabilities by $10,000, so the amount in the equity account must also decrease by $10,000. In essence, the owner has withdrawn some of his equity in the business. The related journal entry would look like this:

| Owner's Equity | $10,000 | |
| Cash | | $10,000 |

Finally, assume that the company repays the $21,000 it borrowed to purchase the land. The balance sheet would then look like this:

		Liabilities and Owner's Equity	
Cash	$54,000	Liabilities	$0
		Owner's Equity	54,000
Total Assets	$54,000	Total Liabilities and Owner's Equity	$54,000

The Cash account is reduced by $21,000, the amount of cash used to repay the loan. (To simplify things, assume no interest was paid.[5]) As a result of the repayment, the liability, Note Payable, disappears.[6] Since Assets and Liabilities have each been reduced by the same amount, $21,000, the difference between the two is unchanged and the amount in the Owner's Equity account stays the same. The balance sheet continues to balance.

The related entry to the company's accounting journal looks like this:

| Note Payable | $21,000 | |
| Cash | | $21,000 |

T-ACCOUNTS

In addition to making journal entries as each transaction occurs, companies keep a separate record for each particular account (such as Cash or Notes Payable) that shows the balance in that account. That collection of account records is known as the *ledger*. The entries in the journal are transferred to the corresponding accounts in the ledger, a process known as ***posting***.

The ledger accounts are often illustrated using what are known as ***T-accounts***. T-accounts keep a running total of the amount in each account. They are called T-accounts because they're shaped like a "T."[7] As with journal entries, every entry to the left-hand side of one T-account must be matched by a corresponding entry to the right-hand side of *some other* T-account. And the totals of all the T-accounts (although not each individual T-account) must balance. The sum of the left-hand sides of all the T-accounts must equal the sum of the right-hand sides of all the T-accounts.

---

[5] My bank doesn't charge me interest. I assume yours doesn't either.

[6] Ta-da!

[7] And you thought accountants had no imagination.

Consider again the series of transactions we reviewed earlier in this chapter. First, an individual contributes $60,000 cash to a new business. As we saw, two accounts are affected, Cash and Owner's Equity:

Cash			Owner's Equity	
60,000				60,000

The Cash account appears on the left-hand, asset side of the balance sheet. Increases to a left-hand account appear on the left of the T-account. Thus, 60,000 on the left of the Cash T-account indicates an addition of $60,000 to Cash. Owner's Equity appears on the right-hand side of the balance sheet. Increases to a right-hand account appear on the right of the T-account. Thus, 60,000 on the right of the Owner's Equity T-account indicates an increase of $60,000 in Owner's Equity. Note that the total of the left-hand sides equals the total of the right-hand sides.

Next, the company borrows $21,000 from a bank, signing a one-year note, and uses the loan to buy land:

Cash		Land		Note Payable		Owner's Equity	
60,000		*21,000*			*21,000*		60,000

The Land account increases by $21,000. Since Land is an asset account on the left-hand side of the balance sheet, the increase appears on the left side of the T-account. The Note Payable account also increases by $21,000. Since Note Payable is a liability account on the right-hand side of the balance sheet, the increase appears on the right side of the T-account. Again, the total of all the left sides, $81,000, equals the total of all the right sides, $81,000; the T-accounts balance.

Next, the company sells the land for $25,000:

Cash		Land		Note Payable		Owner's Equity	
60,000		21,000			21,000		60,000
25,000			*21,000*				*4,000*

Cash increases by $25,000, the Land account is reduced by its full balance, $21,000, and the Owner's Equity account increases by $4,000, the amount of the profit.[8] If you total all the left sides and all the right sides, you'll see that the T-accounts still balance.

Next, the owner withdraws $10,000 cash from the business:

---

[8] As I said earlier, the actual accounting treatment of this transaction is a little more complicated, but the end result is the same.

Cash		Land		Note Payable		Owner's Equity	
60,000		21,000			21,000		60,000
25,000			21,000				4,000
	10,000					10,000	

Cash is reduced by $10,000, a right-hand entry to the Cash T-account, and Owner's Equity is reduced by $10,000, a left-hand entry to the Owner's Equity T-account.

Finally, the company pays the $21,000 note:

Cash		Land		Note Payable		Owner's Equity	
60,000		21,000			21,000		60,000
25,000			21,000	21,000			4,000
	10,000					10,000	
	21,000						

Cash is reduced by $21,000, a right-hand entry to the Cash T-account, and the Note Payable account is reduced by its full amount, $21,000, a left-hand entry to the Note Payable T-account.

T-accounts keep a running total of what is in each account. To prepare a balance sheet, all you need to do is total the figures in each T-account. To total a T-account, you simply add the numbers on each side of the T, and calculate the difference between the two sides. The difference, which appears on the side of the T-account with the larger number, is the balance in the account. The balances in each of the T-accounts below are identical to the numbers that appear on the final balance sheet we prepared earlier in this chapter:[9]

Cash		Land		Note Payable		Owner's Equity	
60,000		21,000			21,000		60,000
25,000			21,000	21,000			4,000
	10,000	0			0	10,000	
	21,000						54,000
54,000							

If you go back and total the amounts in the T-accounts after each transaction, you'll see that, at each step, the totals match the figures in the corresponding balance sheets we prepared earlier.

---

[9] Accounts with zero balances don't appear on the balance sheet.

THE WAY THE BOOKKEEPING SYSTEM WORKS

The various elements of a company's accounting records that we've discussed in this chapter — the accounting journal, the T-accounts for each item, and the financial statements themselves — are part of what's known as the ***bookkeeping system***. But how do those all fit together? Here's how the sequence works:

1. When a company engages in a financial transaction, that transaction is entered in the accounting journal — the chronological entries of transactions as they happen.

2. At some point, the transactions in the journal are transferred to the appropriate T-accounts. That transfer is easy because things go into the T-accounts just as they appear in the journal. A left-hand entry of $10,000 to Cash in the journal becomes a left-hand entry of $10,000 in the Cash T-account. A right-hand entry of $6,000 to Owner's Equity in the journal becomes a right-hand entry of $6,000 in the Owner's Equity T-account.

3. When the company needs to prepare financial statements, each T-account is totaled and the total for that account is entered on the balance sheet.[10]

---

[10] It's actually more complicated than that because there are a number of temporary accounts that never appear on the balance sheet. Before the balance sheet is prepared, these temporary accounts are closed to (emptied into) other accounts that do appear on the balance sheet.

Key Concepts to Remember

1. Balance sheets balance because of double-entry bookkeeping.

2. Under double-entry bookkeeping, every transaction produces equal and offsetting entries to a person's accounting records. Because of these equal entries, the accounting records always balance, meaning that left and right are always equal.

3. Left-hand entries are called debits. Right-hand entries are called credits.

4. ⎛If an account appears on the left side of the balance sheet (Assets), a left-hand entry indicates an increase in the account and a right-hand entry indicates a reduction in the account.⎤If an account appears on the right side of the balance sheet (Liabilities and Equity), a right-hand entry indicates an increase in the account and a left-hand entry indicates a reduction in the account.

5. The accounting journal is a chronological record of transactions as they occur. Each entry in the accounting journal balances. For each transaction, the total sum of debits equals the total sum of credits.

6. T-accounts keep a running total of the amount in each account.

7. Entries in the accounting journal are periodically transferred to the appropriate T-accounts and the balances in the T-accounts are used to prepare financial statements.

Chapter 6

THE EQUITY SECTION OF THE BALANCE SHEET

"Money is better than poverty, if only for financial reasons."
— *Woody Allen*

INTRODUCTION

The equity section of the balance sheet represents the difference between the assets and liabilities of the business or individual — the net worth:

Equity = Assets − Liabilities.

If the business has more assets than liabilities, the total in the equity section is positive. If the business has more liabilities than assets, the total in the equity section is negative.[1]

Net income increases the amount in the equity section; net losses reduce the amount in the equity section. To understand why, recall from Chapter 3 that revenues are the assets a person or business receives for goods or services and expenses are the assets used up to produce revenues. A person has net income for a period if revenues exceed expenses — to oversimplify just a little, when the value of the assets coming in exceeds the value of the assets going out. Equity, the difference between the person's total assets and total liabilities, increases by the amount of the net income. A person has a net loss for a period if expenses exceed revenues — when the value of the assets coming in is less than the value of the assets going out. Equity decreases by the amount of the net loss.

Investments of additional money or withdrawals of money by the owners of the business also affect the equity account. When the owner invests cash or property in the business, the difference between assets and liabilities increases, so the amount in the Equity account increases by the amount of the contribution. Similarly, when the owner withdraws cash or property from the business, the amount in the Equity account decreases by the amount of the withdrawal.

The appearance and name of the equity section of the balance sheet vary depending on the organizational form of the business. Corporations, partnerships, sole proprietorships, and limited liability companies all present equity differently. You'll learn the differences among these various entities in a Corporations or Business Associations course. Luckily, you don't need all the legal details to understand how they account for equity differently.

---

[1] In accounting, negative numbers are represented by parentheses, as in ($400).

SOLE PROPRIETORSHIPS AND INDIVIDUALS

The simplest accounting for equity is for an individual or a sole proprietorship. A sole proprietorship is a business with only one owner that has not taken the legal steps necessary to form some other kind of organization. The equity section of the balance sheet of an individual or a sole proprietorship is simply one line called *Equity* or *Net Worth*. The balance sheet we prepared for Clara Darrow in Chapter 2 provides a good example of the equity section of an individual's balance sheet.

PARTNERSHIPS AND LIMITED LIABILITY COMPANIES

If the business is a partnership, the owners of the business are called partners, and the equity section is called *Partners' Equity*. In a partnership, a separate equity account is maintained for each partner. Equity may appear as a single line on the balance sheet, but, at least internally, the partnership maintains separate equity accounts for each partner. The equity section of a partnership balance sheet might look something like this:

Partners' Equity	
Partner Jones	$10,000
Partner Smith	5,000
Partner Brown	2,000

When a partner invests cash or property in the business, the amount in *that partner's* equity account increases by the amount of the investment. When a partner withdraws cash or property from the business, the amount in *that partner's* equity account decreases by the amount of the withdrawal.

We have already seen that income or losses affect equity. In a partnership, income is allocated to each partner's equity account according to the percentage of profits to which each partner is entitled (as determined under partnership law). Losses are allocated to each partner's account according to each partner's responsibility for losses (again, as determined under partnership law). For example, if the net income of the partnership is $10,000, and the partnership agreement provides that Jones will receive 50% of the profits, Smith 25%, and Brown 25%, the equity section in the example above would change to the following:

Partners' Equity	
Partner Jones	$15,000
Partner Smith	7,500
Partner Brown	4,500

The amount in Jones's equity account increases by $5,000, 50% of the profits. The amounts in Smith's and Brown's equity accounts increase by $2,500 each, since each is entitled to 25% of the profits.

The equity of another popular type of business entity, the limited liability company, is treated like that of a partnership, except for a slight change in terminology. The investors in a limited liability company are known as members, so the title of the equity section on the balance sheet is *Members' Equity*. As in a partnership, a limited liability company maintains a separate equity account for each member.

CORPORATIONS

Equity is more complicated when the business is organized as a corporation. Equity investments in a corporation are represented by shares of stock. When a person invests in a corporation, he receives shares of the corporation's stock and is known as a shareholder or stockholder. The corporate equity section is called *Shareholders' Equity* or *Stockholders' Equity*.

Unlike partnerships, corporations do not create a separate equity account for each investor. A corporation does, however, have more than one equity account. Corporations usually separate the equity portion of the balance sheet into at least three accounts. Accountants and everyone else in the world other than lawyers call those accounts: (1) *Capital Stock* or *Common Stock*,[2] (2) *Additional Paid-in Capital* or *Paid-in Capital in Excess of Par Value*, and (3) *Retained Earnings*. Lawyers and legislators, in their unending quest to be unintelligible, sometimes give different names to these accounts. The following table shows the accounting names of the corporate equity accounts and their legal equivalents:

Corporate Equity Accounts

ACCOUNTING NAME	LEGAL NAME
Capital Stock or Common Stock	Stated Capital
Additional Paid-in Capital or Paid-in Capital in Excess of Par Value	Capital Surplus
Retained Earnings	Earned Surplus

Capital Stock and Additional Paid-in Capital

The amounts in the Capital Stock and Additional Paid-in Capital accounts are based on the price at which the corporation sells its stock to investors. When a company sells its stock, the total added to the two accounts is the total sales price. A corporation that sells 10,000 shares of stock to the public for $50 per share receives $500,000. This $500,000 is allocated between the Capital Stock and Additional Paid-in Capital accounts.[3]

How much of that $500,000 goes into each account depends on whether the stock has a *par value*. Par value is a rather arbitrary value assigned to each type of stock by the corporation that is less (usually significantly less) than the price for which the corporation sells the stock. Depending on the jurisdiction and the desires of the corporation, a corporation's stock may or may not have a par value. For our purposes,

---

[2] Corporations often have two or more types, or classes, of stock. If so, there is a separate account for each class, each with a name that describes the class — such as Class A Stock, Class B Stock, and so on. The name on the account is the same as the name the corporation gives that class of stock.

[3] The balance sheet will still balance because the $500,000 of cash received by the company would be added to the asset, Cash, on the left-hand side of the balance sheet.

you don't have to be familiar with the concept of par value. It's just important that you understand that some stock has a par value and some does not.

If the stock sold has a par value, you add the par value of each share sold to the Capital Stock account. You add the rest of the purchase price to the Additional Paid-in Capital account, which explains this account's alternative name, Paid-in Capital in Excess of Par Value. Assume, for example, that an investor pays a total of $300 cash for three shares of stock with a $10 per share par value. The following changes would occur on the balance sheet:

Assets	*Equity*
Cash + $300	Capital Stock + $30
	Additional Paid-in Capital + $270

The corporation has $300 more cash as a result of the sale, and this is reflected on the asset side of the balance sheet. The aggregate par value of the three shares ($10 × 3 = $30) is added to the Capital Stock account. The remaining $270 of the purchase price is added to the Additional Paid-in Capital account. The journal entry for this transaction would look like this:

Cash		$300
Capital Stock	$30	
Additional Paid-in Capital	$270	

Some stock, called *no-par* stock, has no stated par value. In that case, the amount to be allocated to each account when stock is sold is usually left to the discretion of the corporation's board of directors. The amount allocated to the Capital Stock account can't be called par value because there is no par value, so it is called *stated value*. The amount of the purchase price above the stated value is allocated to the Additional Paid-in Capital account, which in these circumstances is sometimes called *Paid-in Capital in Excess of Stated Value*. If the corporation does not make an allocation decision for no-par stock, the entire price is allocated to the Capital Stock account.

Retained Earnings

The third corporate capital account is **Retained Earnings**. The Retained Earnings account, unlike the other capital accounts, has nothing to do with a company's sales of stock. The figure in the Retained Earnings account results primarily from the cumulative profits and losses of the corporation. If the business has net income, its excess of assets over liabilities increases, and the amount in the Retained Earnings account must increase by the amount of the income. If the business has a net loss, its excess of assets over liabilities decreases, and the amount in the Retained Earnings account must decline by the amount of the loss.

The Retained Earnings total may be a negative number. Accountants usually indicate a negative number by bracketing the number with parentheses. Thus, ($2,000) indicates a negative $2,000. When the Retained Earnings account has a negative balance, it is usually called **Accumulated Deficit**.

Let's consider an example. Assume that the balance sheet of a newly created company looks like this:

Assets		Liabilities and Shareholders' Equity	
Cash	$ 1,000	*Liabilities*	
Building	10,000	Note Payable	$5,000
Equipment	2,000	*Shareholder's Equity*	
		Capital Stock	500
		Additional Paid-in Capital	7,500
		Retained Earnings	0
TOTAL	$13,000	TOTAL	$13,000

We know from the amounts in the Capital Stock and Additional Paid-in Capital accounts that the company sold its stock for $8,000, $500 of which is the stock's cumulative par value. The Notes Payable account tells us that the company also borrowed $5,000. Looking at the asset side of the balance sheet, we see that the company has used most of the cash it received from selling stock and borrowing to purchase a building for $10,000 and equipment for $2,000.

Assume that the company's first year is profitable; it has a net income of $7,500. (To make it simpler, let's assume that its income was all in cash.) The company uses $5,000 of its earnings to repay the note and keeps the remaining $2,500. Its balance sheet now looks like this:

Assets		Liabilities and Shareholders' Equity	
Cash	$ 3,500	*Liabilities*	$0
Building	10,000	*Shareholder's Equity*	
Equipment	2,000	Capital Stock	500
		Additional Paid-in Capital	7,500
		Retained Earnings	7,500
TOTAL	$15,500	TOTAL	$15,500

As the result of the net income, the excess of assets over liabilities increased by $7,500. The Retained Earnings account increased by $7,500 to reflect that income.

The following year is disastrous for the corporation; it has a net loss of $10,000. The $3,500 cash the corporation had on hand at the end of the first year is gone and the corporation had to borrow $6,500 from the bank just to pay its bills. Its balance sheet now looks like this:

Assets		Liabilities and Shareholders' Equity	
Cash	$ 0	*Liabilities*	
Building	10,000	Note Payable	$6,500
Equipment	2,000	*Shareholder's Equity*	
		Capital Stock	500
		Additional Paid-in Capital	7,500
		Accumulated Deficit	(2,500)
TOTAL	$12,000	TOTAL	$12,000

As a result of the loss, the excess of assets over liabilities fell by $10,000. The Retained Earnings account was reduced by $10,000 to reflect that loss. Since the previous Retained Earnings balance was only $7,500, the balance is now a negative $2,500, with the negative balance indicated by the use of parentheses. Since the balance is negative, the account is now called "Accumulated Deficit" rather than "Retained Earnings."

The Capital Stock and Additional Paid-in Capital accounts are unchanged. All accounting profits and losses are reflected in the Retained Earnings account so that the other two accounts continue to reflect the amounts paid for the corporation's stock.

Dividends paid by the corporation also affect the equity accounts. Dividends, for those unfamiliar with the term, are distributions to the shareholders, usually made from the earnings of the business. Dividends are one of the ways a corporation gets the profits of the business to the shareholders.

When a cash dividend is paid, two changes occur. First, the amount in the Cash account is reduced by the amount paid. Second, the amount in the Retained Earnings account is reduced by the amount of the dividend. The key to remembering this is to focus on the word "retained" in Retained Earnings; once those earnings are distributed to the stockholders, they are no longer "retained" by the corporation.

STATEMENT OF CHANGES IN EQUITY

The financial statements of businesses usually contain an accounting statement called something like the ***Statement of Capital Changes***, the ***Statement of Changes in Equity***, or (in the case of a corporation) the ***Statement of Stockholders' Equity***. This statement tracks changes in the equity accounts over the accounting periods covered by the statement. The following is a simple example of such a statement:

STATEMENT OF STOCKHOLDERS' EQUITY
For the Years 2012 and 2013
(All numbers are in millions)

	Common Stock	Addt'l Paid-In Capital	Retained Earnings
Balance as of Jan. 1, 2012	25	175	100
Net Income (or Loss)			40
Common Stock Dividends			(25)
Common Stock Issued	10	70	
Balance as of Dec. 31, 2012	35	245	115
Net Income (or Loss)			(10)
Common Stock Dividends			(15)
Common Stock Repurchased	(5)	(35)	
Balance as of Dec. 31, 2013	30	210	90

This statement shows changes to the company's equity accounts in both 2012 and 2013. The first line of the statement indicates the balance in the company's capital accounts as of January 1, 2012 — the starting point. The Common Stock balance was $25 million, the Additional Paid-in Capital balance was $175 million, and there was $100 million in Retained Earnings.

The next three lines show changes to these accounts during 2012. The "Net Income" line indicates that, in 2012, the company's net income was $40 million; the Retained Earnings account increased by this amount. The company paid dividends to its shareholders of $25 million. This reduced the amount in the Retained Earnings account. The "Common Stock Issued" line shows that the company issued additional common stock for $80 million; $10 million of that amount was allocated to Common Stock, with the remainder allocated to Additional Paid-in Capital.

As a result of the changes, the balances at the end of 2012, represented by the fifth line of the statement, were $35 million in Capital Stock, $245 million in Additional Paid-in Capital, and $115 million in Retained Earnings.

The subsequent lines on the statement show changes to the equity accounts in 2013. The company had a net loss of $10 million in 2013, reducing the balance in Retained Earnings by that amount. The company paid $15 million in dividends, further reducing the amount in Retained Earnings. The company also repurchased some of its stock from its shareholders. The Capital Stock and Additional Paid-in Capital accounts have been reduced to reflect that this stock is no longer outstanding. The final line of the statement indicates the equity account balances as of the end of 2013: $30 million in Capital Stock, $210 million in Additional Paid-in Capital, and $90 million in Retained Earnings.

Key Concepts to Remember

1. Equity = Assets − Liabilities. Net income, by increasing this difference, results in an increase in equity. A net loss, by reducing this difference, results in a reduction in equity.

2. The equity of an individual or sole proprietorship is called Net Worth or just Equity.

3. The equity of a partnership is called Partners' Equity, and includes a separate account for each partner. The equity of a limited liability company is called Members' Equity and includes a separate account for each member.

4. The Equity section of a corporation's balance sheet is split into at least three accounts: (1) Capital Stock or Common Stock, (2) Additional Paid-in Capital or Paid-in Capital in Excess of Par Value, and (3) Retained Earnings. Legal sources sometimes call these accounts Stated Capital, Capital Surplus, and Earned Surplus, respectively.

5. The Capital Stock account is the total par value of stock sold by the corporation. The Additional Paid-in Capital account is the excess of the price of the stock sold over its par value.

6. The Retained Earnings account includes the cumulative income and losses of the corporation, and is reduced when cash dividends are paid to shareholders.

7. The Statement of Changes in Equity, sometimes called the Statement of Capital Changes or the Statement of Stockholders' Equity, shows how the equity accounts changed over a specified accounting period.

Chapter 7

INSOLVENCY

"I'm going to declare moral bankruptcy . . . I mean, we keep using the term in that sense, why not follow it through? When a man can no longer discharge his financial obligations, we let him off the hook. Why not when he can no longer meet his ethical ones? . . . I'm going to pay everybody so much on the dollar. . . . The absolute maximum disbursement I can manage is, roughly, fifty cents on the dollar. Put in plain English, this means that in the future I shall be half the husband I was, half the father, half the friend, and so on down the line."
— *Peter de Vries*

TWO TYPES OF INSOLVENCY

You've probably heard of **insolvency**. You know it's a bad thing financially. But, if you're like most lawyers and law students, that's as far as your understanding goes — unless, like some law students, you've experienced it firsthand.

"Insolvent" is a technical accounting term meaning you're broke. Unfortunately, when you take a simple term like "broke" and transfer it into accounting terms, it gets a little more complicated. Insolvency has at least two different meanings to accountants.[1] With the benefit of this absolutely fantastic introduction to accounting principles,[2] you can now understand the different ways to be broke.[3]

One type of insolvency, **balance sheet insolvency**, focuses on the balance sheet, and compares the total dollar amount of assets to the total dollar amount of liabilities. If total liabilities on the balance sheet exceed total assets, the total of the equity accounts is negative, and the person or business is insolvent in the balance sheet sense. If total assets exceed total liabilities, the total of the equity accounts is positive, and the person or business is solvent.

The second type of insolvency, **cash flow insolvency**, focuses on a person's cash flow and asks whether the person has sufficient cash to pay his obligations as they become due. A person who has sufficient funds to pay his debts as they become due is solvent in this cash flow sense. A person who has insufficient funds to pay his debts as they become due is insolvent.

In your studies, you may encounter the term "equity insolvency." In spite of the use of the word "equity," this is *not* balance sheet insolvency, but cash flow insolvency. The

---

[1] Leave it to accountants to figure out more ways for people to be broke.

[2] Rush out and buy copies for your friends and relatives before they're all gone! Don't worry; I'll wait.

[3] One way would be to rush out and buy more copies of this book than you can afford.

"equity" in equity insolvency is derived from courts of equity, not the section of the balance sheet.

EXAMPLES

The following two examples may make the difference between balance sheet insolvency and cash flow insolvency clearer.[4]

Consider first the balance sheet of Sam Smith:

Assets		Liabilities and Net Worth	
Cash	$100	Liabilities	
Car	20,000	Short-Term Debt	$30,000
House	150,000	Net Worth	140,100
Total Assets	$170,100	Total Liabilities and Net Worth	$170,100

Sam is solvent in the balance sheet, or equity, sense. His total assets, $170,100, are significantly greater than his total liabilities, $30,000, leaving a positive net worth of $140,100.

Sam may not be solvent in the cash flow sense. Sam owes $30,000 in short-term debt (debt due in the near future) and has only $100 cash available to pay it. Sam's cash shortage may be temporary; he might expect to receive $30,000 cash before the debt is due. If so, Sam's not insolvent in the cash flow sense; he will have cash sufficient to pay the debt when it becomes due. If Sam doesn't expect to receive any cash before the debt is due, he still might be able to pay the debt by selling his house or car or borrowing money. But it takes time to sell a house and the debt might be due before Sam could complete the sale. And he might not be able to find anyone willing to lend him money. If Sam can't come up with enough cash to pay the debt when it becomes due, Sam is insolvent in the cash flow sense.

Now consider a person who is in exactly the opposite situation from Sam — insolvent in the balance sheet sense but not in the cash flow sense. Assume that Joe Jones has the following balance sheet:

Assets		Liabilities and Net Worth	
Cash	$20,000	Liabilities	
Car	15,000	Short-Term Debt	$10,000
		Long-Term Debt	50,000
		Net Worth	(25,000)
Total Assets	$35,000	Total Liabilities and Net Worth	$35,000

---

[4] Or they may not. I disclaim all warranties, express or implied.

Joe is insolvent in the balance sheet sense. His total assets, $35,000, are less than his total liabilities, $60,000, resulting in a negative figure in the Equity account.[5]

Joe may not be insolvent in the cash flow sense. He only owes $10,000 in the short term, and he has $20,000 cash available, more than enough to pay that debt. Joe does not presently have enough cash to pay the $50,000 long-term debt, but, since it's long-term debt, he doesn't have to pay it now. The only issue is whether he will have enough cash to pay this debt when it becomes due. If Joe expects to receive sufficient cash by the time the debt is due, he is not insolvent in the cash flow sense.

Notice how much easier it is to determine balance sheet insolvency than it is to determine cash flow insolvency. Determining balance sheet insolvency only requires a quick look at the balance sheet. Cash flow insolvency, on the other hand, requires judgment. You can't just look at a financial statement. You have to consider when debts are due and when the person expects to receive cash and in what amounts, and make a prediction.

THE INSOLVENCIES OF LAW STUDENTS

Many law students get to experience the joys of both cash flow insolvency and balance sheet insolvency. During law school, many law students find it hard to come up with sufficient cash to pay their bills on time. They are insolvent or nearly insolvent in the cash flow sense. By the time they exit law school, many law students are insolvent in the balance sheet sense. Because of the substantial debt they incurred to go to law school, their liabilities exceed their assets (because the law degree isn't treated as a balance sheet asset). They have a negative net worth. But, if they are lucky enough to find a good legal job on graduation, they're probably no longer insolvent in the cash flow sense. The income they will receive from working 100 billable hours a week as associates at high-priced law firms will be more than enough to pay their law school debts as they become due.[6]

Key Concepts to Remember

1. A company or person can be insolvent in two different senses.

2. A person is insolvent in the balance sheet sense if his liabilities exceed his assets — in other words, if the total of the equity accounts is negative.

3. A person is insolvent in the cash flow sense if she has insufficient cash to pay her debts as they become due.

---

[5] You do remember that accountants indicate negatives with parentheses, don't you? And no, the value of this book should not be in parentheses.

[6] If, on the other hand, they're working as assistant managers at McDonald's because they couldn't find a law-related job, they may still be insolvent in the cash flow sense. Their income may be insufficient to repay their student loans and they'll use what they learned in that bankruptcy course sooner than they expected.

Section Three

ACCRUAL, DEFERRAL, AND CASH FLOW

Chapter 8

ACCRUAL AND DEFERRAL

"Y'see . . . [accounting's] . . . sort of a game with me. Its whole object is to prove that two plus two equals four. That seems to make sense, but you'd be surprised at the number of people who try to stretch it to five."
— *Dalton Trumbo*

TWO METHODS OF ACCOUNTING

Every expense paid in advance creates what is in essence an asset. When a company pays its May rent in February, it creates a claim to occupy the rented space in May, an asset that will be used in the future. That asset may not last for very long, but it is nevertheless an asset.

Conversely, almost every asset is in essence a prepaid expense. When a company buys a truck that will last for twenty years, it has paid in advance for transportation for the next twenty years. The cost of the truck is an expense of producing income in all those future periods.

Payments for expenses and for the purchase of assets could be accounted for in two very different ways: on a *cash basis* or on an *accrual basis*. Both methods are ways of determining a company's net income; the difference between them is one of timing. Net income, you will recall, is measured for a particular period: the income statement presents a person's income for a specified period of time, such as a year. The cash basis of accounting and the accrual basis of accounting allocate revenues and expenses to particular accounting periods in different ways.

THE CASH BASIS OF ACCOUNTING

Accountants ordinarily use the accrual basis, but the best way to understand the accrual basis is to contrast it with the cash basis. The *cash basis* of accounting focuses on when cash changes hands. It allocates revenues to the accounting period in which cash is received and allocates expenses to the period in which cash is paid. It doesn't matter when the company actually delivers the goods to the customer or performs the services. When a customer pays, the cash payment is allocated to revenue and increases the company's net income for that period.

Similarly, an expense is charged against income when the company pays it. It doesn't matter when the company receives the benefit of the payment. If, on January 2, 2014, a company pays $30,000 for a truck, the entire $30,000 would be treated as an expense in January, 2014. All that matters using the cash basis is when cash changes hands.

THE ACCRUAL BASIS OF ACCOUNTING

If you're using the **accrual basis** of accounting, the recognition of revenues and expenses doesn't depend on when cash is received or paid. In the accrual system, revenues are usually recognized when the seller substantially completes whatever he is doing to earn the money. This idea is known as the **revenue recognition principle**.

If the company's selling goods, revenues are usually recognized when the goods are delivered to the buyer. If the company's providing services, revenues are usually recognized when the services are substantially performed. It doesn't matter whether the customer has paid for those goods or services yet. If, for example, the company delivers goods to a customer in 2014, the revenue is recognized in 2014, even if the customer doesn't pay until 2015.

Similarly, in the accrual system, expenses are charged against income in the period when those expenses provide benefits, not when they are paid. Expenses are usually recognized when the revenue to which those expenses relate is recognized. This rule is known as the **matching principle** because you match the expense to the corresponding revenue. For example, a company would recognize the cost of goods it sold as an expense in the same period it recognized the revenue from selling those goods. If an expense doesn't easily match to any particular revenue but that expense is periodic, like interest or rent, it's recognized in the period it relates to. For example, if a company prepays five years of rent, one-fifth of the payment is treated as an expense in each of the five years.

In the accrual system, revenue and expenses may be **accrued** or **deferred**. Allocating revenue or expenses to the income statement *before cash changes hands* (before the cash is collected in the case of revenues or before the cash is paid in the case of expenses) is known as **accrual**. In essence, accrual pulls future payments into the present. Allocating revenues or expenses to the income statement in a period *after the period in which cash changes hands* (after the cash is collected in the case of revenue or after the cash is paid in the case of expenses) is known as **deferral**. In essence, deferral pushes present payments into the future. Although the method is known as the accrual method, it includes both accrual and deferral.

Most large or mid-sized businesses use the accrual method of accounting, but many individuals and professionals (such as doctors and lawyers) use the cash method. Your checkbook uses the cash method. You enter checks in your checkbook when you send them, not when you think the payment will benefit you.[1] Accountants believe the accrual method provides a more accurate picture because it better matches revenues and expenses to the appropriate period.

EXAMPLES OF ACCRUAL AND DEFERRAL

Here are some examples of accrual and deferral:

1. Accrued Revenue. A lawyer completes work on a case and sends the client a bill on November 15, 2013, but the client does not pay until February 1, 2014. The lawyer's

---

[1] If you don't write them down at all, you have bigger problems than not knowing accounting.

work was done and the fee earned as of November 15, 2013, but the cash was not received until the following year. Using the cash basis of accounting, the fee would be revenue in the year 2014, when the client paid. Using the accrual basis, the fee is accrued and treated as revenue in 2013, the year the work was completed, even though the lawyer did not collect until 2014.

2. Accrued Expense. A lawyer orders one month's supply of legal pads on October 1, 2013. The pads are delivered to the lawyer in October and are gone by the end of the year. However, the lawyer doesn't pay the bill for the legal pads until January 10, 2014. Using the cash basis of accounting, the cost of the legal pads would be an expense in 2014, the year the bill was paid. Using the accrual basis, the cost of the pads is an expense in 2013, when the legal pads were used to help the lawyer produce revenue. The expense is accrued to 2013.

3. Deferred Revenue. On October 12, 2013, a client pays a lawyer a cash fee of $1,000 to represent the client at a hearing in March, 2014. The lawyer does no work on the case in 2013, but represents the client at the hearing in March. Using the cash basis of accounting, the fee would be revenue in the year the lawyer received the cash, 2013. Using the accrual basis, the fee is not revenue until 2014, when the lawyer did the work and earned the fee. The revenue is deferred until 2014.

4. Deferred Expense. In 2014, a lawyer prepays his office rent for the next six years. Using the cash basis of accounting, the entire rent payment would be an expense in 2014, the year it was paid. Using the accrual basis, the rent payment is allocated over the next six years. The expense is deferred to the periods when the benefit of the rent payment is received.

ACCOUNTING FOR ACCRUAL AND DEFERRAL ITEMS

That's what accrual accounting is, but how does it work in practice? What bookkeeping entries have to be made and when?

1. Deferred Revenues

When revenue is deferred, the business has received the cash, but it will not be recognized as revenue until a later accounting period. Assume that a business has received $100 cash for work it has not yet performed. The $100 has not yet been earned, so the income must be deferred to a later accounting period.

Obviously, the receipt of the cash increases the Cash account by $100. The offsetting entry cannot be to Revenue, because the revenue is not to be recognized in this accounting period. Instead, the $100 is added to an account with a name like Unearned Revenue or Deferred Revenue. This account appears in the liability section of the balance sheet because the company is obligated to do something before the income is earned. Thus, the balance sheet changes as follows:

Assets		*Liabilities and Equity*	
Cash	+$100	Unearned or Deferred Revenue	+$100

When this income is earned by performance, the unearned or deferred revenue account is reduced by the $100, and $100 is added to revenue for that period.

2. Deferred Expenses

When an expense is deferred, the business has paid cash, but the payment will not be recognized as an expense until some future period. Assume, for example, that in 2014 a business pays $5,000 for its 2015 rent. One of the accounting entries is obvious: the Cash account must be reduced by $5,000 because the business now has $5,000 less cash. But what is the offsetting entry so the books continue to balance? In essence, the business has a new asset that it will use sometime in the future — the ability to occupy the rented space in 2015. A new asset account called Prepaid Rent or Deferred Rent Expense is created, and $5,000 is added to this account.

In 2015, the $5,000 will be recognized as an expense. At that time, the $5,000 is moved from the Prepaid Rent account to a Rent Expense account that is used in calculating net income for the year.

3. Accrued Revenues

When revenue is accrued, the business has earned the revenue by substantially completing the work, but the customer has not yet paid. Assume that in 2014, a company performed services for a customer and billed the customer for the agreed charge of $300, but the customer did not pay by the end of the year. The $300 will be recognized as revenue in 2014, so the $300 must be added to a Revenue account (a right-hand account). The company has not received any cash, but it does have the right to receive the money, and this right is an asset. The offsetting entry is to create an asset account called Accounts Receivable (or perhaps Accrued Revenue Receivable), and to add the $300 to that account.

When the customer pays for the work, the business moves the $300 from Accounts Receivable (or Accrued Revenue Receivable) to Cash. Upon payment, the asset is no longer the right to receive the $300 (Accounts Receivable), but the actual cash itself (Cash). Revenues aren't affected by the payment because the $300 has already been recognized as revenue.

4. Accrued Expenses

When an expense is accrued, the business has received the economic benefit of the expense, but has not yet paid for it. Assume, for example, that a business rented an office in 2014, but did not pay the $7,000 bill until 2015. The $7,000 will be recognized as an expense in calculating 2014 income, so $7,000 is added to the Rent Expense account. But what is the offsetting entry? The business is obligated to pay the rent; in other words, it has a liability. The $7,000 is added to a liability account with a name like Rent Expense Payable, or Rent Payable.

When the rent is paid, the amount of the payment is subtracted from the Cash account and the $7,000 Rent Payable is eliminated because the liability no longer exists — it's been paid. Expenses aren't affected by the payment because the $7,000 has already been recognized as an expense.

5. *Summary*

The following table summarizes how accrual and deferral items are treated on the accounting records of the business:

DEFERRED REVENUE	*When Cash Received*	*When Recognized*
	Cash +	Revenue +
	Unearned or Deferred	Unearned or Deferred
	Revenue +	Revenue −
DEFERRED EXPENSE	*When Cash Paid*	*When Recognized*
	Cash −	Expense +
	Prepaid or Deferred	Prepaid or Deferred
	Expense +	Expense −
ACCRUED REVENUE	*When Recognized*	*When Cash Received*
	Receivable +	Cash +
	Revenue +	Receivable −
ACCRUED EXPENSE	*When Recognized*	When Cash *Paid*
	Expense +	Cash −
	Payable +	Payable −

Key Concepts to Remember

1. There are two basic accounting methods: the cash method and the accrual method. For most purposes, accountants use the accrual method.

2. The cash method recognizes revenues and expenses when cash changes hands — when the company receives payment and when it pays its bills.

3. The accrual method recognizes revenues when they are earned by the sale of goods or the performance of services, not when the customer pays. Expenses are recognized when the associated revenue is recognized or, in the case of periodic expenses like rent or interest, in the periods the rent or interest covers.

4. Allocating revenue or expenses to the income statement before the cash changes hands (before the cash is collected in the case of revenues or before the cash is paid in the case of expenses) is known as accrual. In essence, accrual pulls future payments into the present.

5. Allocating revenues or expenses to the income statement after the period in which cash changes hands (after the cash is collected in the case of revenue or after the cash is paid in the case of expenses) is known as deferral. In essence, deferral pushes present payments into the future.

6. Although the method is known as the accrual method, it includes both accrual and deferral.

Chapter 9

DEPRECIATION, DEPLETION, AND AMORTIZATION

"Never call an accountant a credit to his profession. A good accountant is a debit to his profession."
— *Charles J. C. Lyall*

THE BASIC CONCEPT: ALLOCATING THE COST OF CAPITAL ASSETS

Many assets that a company purchases will provide benefits over several accounting periods. A company's truck, for example, will last for several years and help produce income throughout its life. It wouldn't be accurate to treat the entire cost of the truck as an expense when it is purchased; that period's income is not the only income the truck will help to produce. Instead, the cost of the truck should be spread as an expense over all the years it helps the company produce income.[1]

The allocation of the cost of such long-lived assets (sometimes called capital assets) over several accounting periods is called ***depreciation, depletion***, or ***amortization.*** When the asset is plant or equipment, the term depreciation is used. When the asset is a natural resource, like oil, gas, or timber, the term depletion is used. When the asset is an intangible, like a patent, the term amortization is used. In spite of the different names, the basic accounting idea is the same: to allocate the cost of the asset as an expense over several accounting periods.

The point of depreciation, depletion, and amortization is to spread the cost of an asset over its useful life, not to reflect the actual deterioration of the asset or the actual decline in its market value. The horse-drawn buggy the company bought in 1880 may be fully depreciated, but it is not necessarily worthless. It may be an extremely valuable antique. Conversely, because of technological change, the computer the company bought two years ago may be worth less than the amount on the company's balance sheet. Always remember that the balance sheet, or book, value of an asset is not necessarily its market value.

The cost of one familiar long-lived asset, land, is not allocated in this way. The costs of structures and equipment on land are depreciated, and the costs of natural resources on or under land are depleted, but the cost of the land itself is not usually allocated as an expense. Land, like love, is forever.[2] In addition, special rules apply to intangible assets, so their costs may not always be amortized over the useful life of the

---

[1] This is, of course, just another example of deferral.

[2] So, when your boyfriend asks how you feel about him, tell him you land him. It's just as good.

asset, but those special rules are beyond the scope of this book.

THE EFFECT OF DEPRECIATION ON THE ACCOUNTING STATEMENTS

Depreciation (and depletion and amortization) affect both the income statement and the balance sheet. Depreciation affects the income statement because it is an expense which reduces net income. Depreciation affects the balance sheet in two ways, one direct and one indirect. The direct effect is that depreciation reduces the balance sheet value of the asset being depreciated. The indirect effect of depreciation on the balance sheet results from its effect on income. Depreciation, an expense, reduces net income, and the amount of net income affects the equity section of the balance sheet. Thus, depreciation indirectly reduces equity.[3]

Depreciation does not affect a company's cash flow in any way. Although depreciation is an expense, no cash payment is made for depreciation. Depreciation merely allocates as an expense the amount *previously paid* for an asset when it was acquired. Similarly, the process of depreciation provides no cash to purchase a new asset when the old one wears out. A company is not required to set aside cash, as an asset is depreciated, to eventually replace the asset. Depreciation is only a bookkeeping entry.

THE BALANCE SHEET TREATMENT OF DEPRECIATION

The balance sheet often shows the original cost of an asset, the total amount of depreciation allocated to it over the years, and the difference between the two. The original cost of an asset is known as its **basis**. The cumulative amount of depreciation is known as **accumulated depreciation**. The difference between the original cost of an asset and its accumulated depreciation is known as the asset's **book value**.

Assume that a company bought some equipment two years ago for $30,000. If the company's annual depreciation expense for the equipment is $1,500, after two years the Equipment entry on the balance sheet would look like this:

Equipment	$30,000	
Less: Accumulated Depreciation	(3,000)	$27,000

The $30,000 figure is the original cost. After two years, the accumulated depreciation is $3,000 ($1,500 × 2 years). The book value is the difference between these two figures, $27,000.

METHODS OF CALCULATING DEPRECIATION

The Straight-Line Method

Several different methods of calculating depreciation are acceptable. The easiest method is the **straight-line** method. Under the straight-line method, the cost of the

---

[3] And, since you're reducing numbers on each side of the balance sheet by the same amount, the balance sheet continues to balance. Accountants are such miracle workers!

asset is allocated equally over its useful life.

For example, assume that a company pays $15,500 for a truck that it expects to use for 5 years. At the end of five years, the truck will be useless to the company, but can be sold to a junkyard for its scrap value of $500. This $500 is known as the truck's *residual or salvage value*. Salvage value is simply the value of an asset at the end of its useful life to the company. The difference between the cost of the truck and its salvage value is known as the *depreciable cost*. The depreciable cost of the truck is $15,500 − $500 = $15,000.

The straight-line method allocates the depreciable cost of the asset evenly over its useful life. Using the straight-line method, the annual depreciation will be $15,000 ÷ 5 = $3,000 each year. In other words, 1/5, or 20% of the depreciable cost of the truck is depreciated each year. After five years, the truck is fully depreciated, and no further depreciation is taken, even if the truck is still in use.

The journal entry each year would look like this:

Depreciation Expense	$3,000	
Accumulated Depreciation: Truck		$3,000

The left-hand entry is to Depreciation Expense to recognize that portion of the truck's cost as an expense for the year. The right-hand entry is to the balance sheet account, Accumulated Depreciation, that will be offset against the truck's historical cost.

The Units-of-Output Method

Another method of depreciation, known as the **units-of-output** method, measures the useful life of an asset in units of output instead of years. For a machine, the appropriate measure of output might be hours of operation. For a truck, the appropriate measure might be miles driven.

Consider the $15,500 truck again. If its useful life is 100,000 miles and its salvage value is $500, then the depreciation expense per mile driven is $15,000 ÷ 100,000 = $0.15 per mile. The amount of depreciation expense in any period would be the number of miles the truck was driven that period times $0.15 per mile. If, for example, the truck was driven 25,000 miles in a year, depreciation expense for that year would be 25,000 × $0.15 = $3,750.

Accelerated Depreciation Methods

Accelerated depreciation methods produce more depreciation expense in the early life of an asset and less in later years. The two primary accelerated depreciation methods are the **declining-balance** method and the **sum-of-the-years'-digits** method.

In the **declining-balance** method, the normal, straight-line rate of depreciation is increased by some factor and the increased rate is applied each year to the *book value* of the asset.[4] For example, the ***double-declining-balance*** method uses a rate twice the straight-line rate. The ***150%-declining-balance*** method uses a rate 1½ times the straight-line rate.[5]

Assume again that a company pays $15,500 for a truck with a useful life of 5 years. As we previously saw, the straight-line method would depreciate 20% (1/5) of the $15,000 depreciable cost each year. The double-declining-balance method doubles this rate to 40%, and applies that rate to the asset's book value at the beginning of that year (without first subtracting the salvage value).

Depreciation of the truck for the first year would be $15,500 x .40 = $6,200. The ***book value*** of the truck (the net value on the balance sheet, after subtracting depreciation) at the end of the first year would be $15,500 − $6,200 = $9,300. Depreciation for the second year would be $9,300 x .40 = $3,720. The book value of the truck at the end of the second year would be $9,300 − $3,720 = $5,580. Depreciation of the truck would continue at the same 40% rate until the book value is equal to the truck's salvage value. At that point, no further depreciation expense would be taken.

The ***sum-of-the-years'-digits*** method is more complicated. The depreciation rate is a fraction. The numerator of the fraction (if you're one of those students who came to law school to escape math, that's the top part) is the number of years of useful life remaining at the *beginning* of the year. The denominator of the fraction (the bottom part) is the sum of the years of useful life; the denominator is the same every year.

Returning to our truck example, the denominator of the fraction is the sum of the five years of useful life, $1 + 2 + 3 + 4 + 5 = 15$. The numerator for the first year's depreciation would be 5, since, at the beginning of the first year, when the truck is first acquired, the truck has 5 years of expected useful life. The fractional rate is applied to the depreciable cost of the asset (the cost less the salvage value). Thus, depreciation in the first year would be 5/15, or one-third, of the $15,000 depreciable cost, which is $5,000. Depreciation in the second year would be 4/15 of the $15,000 cost, which is $4,000. Depreciation would be 3/15 of the $15,000 in the third year, 2/15 in the fourth year, and 1/15 in the fifth and final year. After five years, the truck is fully depreciated and no further depreciation expense is taken.

DEPLETION OF NATURAL RESOURCES

Depletion is the equivalent of depreciation when the asset is a natural resource, like mineral deposits or oil and gas. Depletion is measured by dividing the cost of the natural resource by the estimated total number of available units. Assume, for example, that a company pays $5 million for the oil rights on property estimated to contain 1 million barrels of oil. The cost per barrel is $5 million divided by 1 million barrels, or $5. If the company extracts and sells 150,000 barrels in the first year, the depletion expense for that year is $5 per barrel times 150,000 barrels, or $750,000.

---

[4] This depreciation rate is applied to the full book value of the truck; its salvage value is not subtracted.

[5] And a method I recently invented, the gazillion-declining-balance method, depreciates any asset, no matter how expensive, in a nanosecond.

Depletion, like depreciation, is an expense to be deducted from revenue in calculating net income. Depletion also affects the balance sheet in the same way as depreciation. The original cost of the asset (Oil Reserves in the example) must be reduced on the balance sheet by the amount of the accumulated depletion. After the first year's depletion, the entry for Oil Reserves on the asset side of the balance sheet would look like this:

Oil Reserves	$5,000,000	
Less: Accumulated Depletion	(750,000)	$4,250,000

AMORTIZATION OF INTANGIBLES

Amortization is the same concept applied to intangible assets, such as patents and trademarks. Amortization allocates the cost of an intangible asset over its useful life. Under special accounting rules applied to intangibles, the cost of intangible assets is not always amortized.[6] But, when intangible assets are amortized, the result is similar to depreciation and depletion.

Assume, for example, that a company purchases a patent for $400,000. It expects the patent to have economic value for 10 years, after which the invention will become obsolete and be of no further value to the company. Using the straight-line method, each year the company will recognize an amortization expense of $40,000 ($400,000 ÷ 10) and reduce the balance sheet value of the patent by $40,000.

---

[6] The cost of intangible assets does not always appear on a company's balance sheet. In some cases, a company may (in some cases, must) treat the full cost of an intangible asset as an immediate expense. *See* Financial Accounting Standards Board, Accounting Standards Codification § 350-25-3. And even some intangible assets that do appear on the balance sheet, such as goodwill, are not amortized. *See* Financial Accounting Standards Board, Accounting Standards Codification § 350-35-1. Believe it or not, it's even more complicated than this footnote, but that's enough for this book.

Key Concepts to Remember

1. Depreciation, depletion, and amortization are all ways of allocating the cost of long-lived assets (capital assets) as expenses over the useful life of the asset. Depreciation is the name used for tangible assets. Depletion is the name used for natural resources. Amortization is the name used for intangible assets.

2. The straight-line method allocates the cost of an asset, less its salvage value, in equal amounts over the asset's useful life. Salvage value is the estimated price for which the company could sell the asset when it's no longer of use to the company.

3. In the double-declining-balance method, the normal, straight-line rate of depreciation is doubled and the doubled rate is applied each period to the book value of the asset. This continues each period until the book value is reduced to the salvage value.

4. The depreciation rate for the sum-of-the-years'-digits method is a fraction. The numerator of the fraction is the number of years of useful life remaining at the beginning of the year. The denominator of the fraction is the sum of the total years of useful life. The depreciation for each year is the cost of the asset, less its salvage value, times the appropriate fraction.

5. Both the cost of an asset and its total accumulated depreciation usually are shown on the balance sheet. The difference is known as the asset's book value.

Chapter 10

INVENTORY

"Whatever is not nailed down is mine. Whatever I can pry loose is not nailed down."
— *Collis P. Huntington*

INTRODUCTION

You probably have heard the phrase "taking inventory," as in, "I'm taking inventory of all the reasons why I should not have come to law school." **Inventory** is the accounting term for the goods a business holds for sale to its customers in the regular course of business.[1] If the company is only a merchandising company (meaning that it sells goods manufactured by others), inventory is the goods available to be sold to customers. When you walk into a department store, all of the items for sale on the shelves are inventory, plus any merchandise the store has stored in the back or in a separate warehouse.[2] The shelves themselves are not inventory because the company doesn't sell them in the regular course of its business.

If the company is a manufacturing company (meaning that it manufactures its own goods for sale), inventory includes more. A manufacturing company has three types of inventory: (1) *raw materials*, (2) *work in process*, and (3) *finished goods. Raw materials* are the materials used to make the goods which the company manufactures. For example, if the company makes steel, the raw materials are the coal, iron, and Acme Instant Steel Mix that the company uses to make the steel.[3] *Work in process* is unfinished goods that the company has begun to make but not yet completed. For example, if the steel company has combined the coal, iron, and Instant Steel Mix in its giant mixing bowl, but it has not yet hardened, this would be work in process. *Finished goods* are the completed goods that are ready for sale; in the case of the steel company, this would be the finished steel.

---

[1] To put it more technically, inventory is the stuff sitting around waiting to be sold.

[2] To impress others with your new accounting sophistication, walk into a busy store and, in your loudest voice, exclaim, "Wow! Look at all the inventory."

[3] Even I realize that steel isn't made with something called Acme Instant Steel Mix. The Japanese drove most American companies, including Acme, out of business in the 1980's. Most steel manufacturers now use Nokamura Instant Steel Mix.

BEGINNING AND ENDING INVENTORY AND THE COST OF GOODS SOLD

A company's inventory changes during each accounting period. The company sells some of its inventory to customers. These sales reduce its inventory. The company may add to its inventory by purchasing more goods to sell or, if it's a manufacturing company, by making more goods to sell.

Beginning Inventory is the inventory on hand for sale at the beginning of an accounting period. ***Ending Inventory*** is the inventory on hand at the end of the same accounting period. The basic inventory equation is:

$$\text{Beginning Inventory} + \text{Inventory Purchased or Manufactured}^4 - \text{Cost of Goods Sold} = \text{Ending Inventory}$$

The accounting value of the inventory at the end of the period (Ending Inventory) is equal to the value of the inventory at the beginning of the period (Beginning Inventory) plus additions to that inventory (Inventory Purchased or Manufactured) minus what was sold (Cost of Goods Sold).[5]

Using a little algebra,[6] this equation becomes:

$$\text{Cost of Goods Sold} = \text{Beginning Inventory} + \text{Inventory Purchased or Manufactured} - \text{Ending Inventory}$$

To compute the cost of the goods that have been sold during the period (the Cost of Goods Sold), you add how much you had at the beginning of the period (Beginning Inventory) to how much you added during the period (Inventory Purchased or Manufactured), and subtract what's left at the end of the period (Ending Inventory). Ignoring the problem of theft, the difference is what you sold.

The ***Cost of Goods Sold*** — the inventory sold during the period — is an expense. Selling those goods produced revenue and the cost of the goods must be subtracted from that revenue to determine the net income or loss arising from the sales.

Companies keep track of inventory and the cost of goods sold in one of two ways, the ***periodic method*** or the ***perpetual method***. The bookkeeping differs depending on which method the company uses, but that's beyond the scope of this book.[7]

---

[4] It's a little more complicated if the company returns some of the inventory it purchased to its supplier. The "inventory purchased" in this formula and the next one is *net purchases* — the amount originally purchased from the supplier less any amount returned to the supplier for a credit (known as *purchase returns or allowances*). If there are any such returns, those need to be subtracted from Inventory Purchased or Manufactured in the formulas.

[5] In more technical accounting lingo, the stuff you have at the end of the period is what you had to start with plus new stuff minus stuff you sold. Only an accounting professional could have figured this one out.

[6] I won't bore you with the algebra because, frankly, I'm not very good at it.

[7] The perpetual method adjusts the inventory account and the cost of goods sold as each item is sold. The periodic method only adjusts the inventory account and determines the cost of goods sold at the end of each period.

INVENTORY ON THE BALANCE SHEET

Inventory is an asset. Like most other assets, it is usually valued on the balance sheet at its cost to the business. The cost of the inventory is the sum of all the expenditures and charges directly or indirectly incurred in bringing the inventory to its present condition and location. If the company is a merchandising company that buys its goods from someone else, the cost is the price it paid for the goods, including any transportation costs it had to pay. If the company is a manufacturing company that makes the goods it sells, the cost is the cost of manufacturing the goods, including the cost of all the raw materials.

Under a complicated accounting rule known as the *lower-of-cost-or-market rule*, a company may sometimes have to reduce the value of its inventory on the balance sheet to below what it paid for it, treating the amount of the write-down as a loss. This rule applies whenever, because of physical damage, deterioration, obsolescence, or a decline in prices, the "market" cost of the goods in inventory has declined since the company acquired them.

"Market" in this rule usually means not the price at which the company can sell the goods, but their *replacement cost* — what it would cost the company at today's prices to purchase or produce the inventory. The lower-of-cost-or-market rule says that, if the replacement cost of the inventory is less than what the inventory actually cost the company (its book value), the value on the balance sheet should be reduced to the market cost — the replacement cost. In other words, you use the lower of the two values, actual cost or replacement cost.

For example, if the Ma Yo-Yo Store bought its yo-yos from the manufacturer for $5 each, but the manufacturer is now selling them for $4, the book value of the yo-yos would have to be reduced to $4 each. A couple of exceptions you don't want to know about complicate this rule,[8] but the basic point is that the book value of inventory will sometimes be less than what the company paid for it. If the book value of inventory is reduced using the lower-of-cost-or-market rule, the amount of the reduction is either treated as an addition to the Cost of Goods Sold for that period or shown separately as a loss on the income statement.

It is important to understand that the lower-of-cost-or-market rule only applies if the market value is *less* than the cost. The lower-of-cost-or-market rule requires a company to *reduce* the book value of its inventory below the inventory's cost; it does not allow a company to *increase* the book value of its inventory if the replacement cost goes up.

INVENTORY AS AN EXPENSE: THE COST OF GOODS SOLD

The Cost of Goods Sold is an expense. When a company sells some of its inventory, it receives revenue. The Cost of Goods Sold is one of the expenses associated with that revenue.

---

[8] If you must know, the "market" figure cannot exceed net realizable value and cannot be less than net realizable value less normal profit. I said you didn't want to know.

Unfortunately, it is not always easy to determine the Cost of Goods Sold. The cost to manufacture or purchase inventory varies over time. When some of the inventory is sold, which of the various possible costs should be used? For example, assume that Acme Corporation sells widgets,[9] all of which are identical. Acme bought its widgets over a period of several years, at various prices ranging from $3 to $6 per widget. When Acme sells one widget, what cost should it use for that widget? Which cost in the $3 to $6 range is its expense?

Several different methods of computing the Cost of Goods Sold are acceptable to accountants. One possibility is what's known as *specific identification*. Acme could keep track of each individual widget and what it cost. It might, for example, put a serial number on each widget that indicates how much Acme paid for it. When Acme sells a widget, the Cost of Goods Sold would be how much the particular widget sold cost Acme.

Specific identification makes sense for some types of goods — particularly goods that are unique and very valuable. An art dealer could keep a record of each valuable painting purchased and, when it is sold, match that expense to the sale. But specific identification doesn't make sense for goods like widgets that are low cost and fungible. Acme doesn't want to keep track of the specific cost of each widget; it may have thousands or even millions of them.[10] Some other method is needed.

Three other methods are commonly used: the *FIFO method*, the *LIFO method*, and the *average cost method*. The *FIFO*[11] *(First-In, First-Out) method* assumes that goods are sold in the order in which the business originally purchased them. The first units of inventory purchased — the ones the business has held the longest — are assumed to be the first ones sold (even if they really aren't). To determine the cost of goods sold, you begin with the cost of the oldest unit in inventory, continue to the next oldest unit, and so on, until the total amount sold has been reached.

The *LIFO*[12] *(Last-In, First-Out) method* assumes that the goods are sold in exactly the opposite of the order in which the business originally purchased them. The units purchased most recently — the ones the business has held the shortest amount of time — are assumed to be the first ones sold. To determine the cost of goods sold, you begin with the cost of the newest unit in inventory, continue to the next most recent unit, and so on, until the total amount sold has been reached.

The *average cost method* averages the costs of all the units in inventory. The total book value of the inventory is divided by the total number of units to produce an average cost per unit. To determine the cost of goods sold, you multiply this average cost by the number of units sold.

---

[9] Business and accounting professors always hypothesize that companies sell widgets. No one knows what a widget is. My dictionary, for example, defines it as "an unnamed or hypothetical manufactured article." THE AMERICAN HERITAGE DICTIONARY OF THE ENGLISH LANGUAGE 2040 (3d ed. 1992). As far as I know, you can only buy widgets in unnamed, hypothetical stores.

[10] It depends on how big the hypothetical warehouse is.

[11] It's pronounced fife-o.

[12] It's pronounced life-o.

An example will illustrate the differences among the FIFO, LIFO, and average cost methods. Assume that Acme's beginning inventory is 100 widgets. Ten of those widgets were acquired in 2011 for $3 each; 30 of those widgets were acquired in 2012 for $4 each; 25 of those widgets were acquired in 2013 for $5 each; and the remaining 35 widgets were acquired in 2014 for $6 each. The following table summarizes these figures:

Year	2011	2012	2013	2014
No. of widgets	10	30	25	35
Cost per widget	$3	$4	$5	$6

The total book value of the widgets is $485 [(10 × $3) + (30 × $4) + (25 × $5) + (35 × $6)]. Assume that, in 2014, Acme sells 62 widgets. Using each method, what is the cost of goods sold and what is the book value of Acme's ending inventory?

The LIFO method assumes that the 62 most recently acquired widgets are the ones that are sold — the 35 that were purchased in 2014, the 25 that were purchased in 2013, and 2 of the 30 that were purchased in 2012. The Cost of Goods Sold is $343 [(35 × $6) + (25 × $5) + (2 × $4)]. The book value of the ending inventory, the difference between the beginning inventory and the cost of goods sold, is $485 − $343 = $142.

The FIFO method assumes that the 62 units sold are the oldest ones in inventory — the 10 that were purchased in 2011, the 30 that were purchased in 2012, and 22 of the 25 that were purchased in 2013. The Cost of Goods Sold is $260 [(10 × $3) + (30 × $4) + (22 × $5)]. The value of the ending inventory, the difference between the total inventory cost and the cost of goods sold, is $485 − $260 = $225.

The average cost method uses average values. The average cost of each widget in inventory is $4.85, the total cost of the inventory, $485, divided by the total number of widgets, 100. The Cost of Goods Sold is this average cost times the number of widgets sold, $4.85 × 62 = $300.70. The value of the ending inventory is the difference between the total inventory cost and the cost of goods sold, $485 − $300.70 = $184.30.

Notice that the inventory method chosen affects both income and the valuation on the balance sheet of the remaining inventory. If costs are rising (an inflationary economy), then inventory purchased more recently cost more than older inventory. In that case, the LIFO method produces a higher Cost of Goods Sold and a lower income than the FIFO method. Since the Closing Inventory on the balance sheet is the inventory remaining unsold, the LIFO method results in a lower inventory value on the balance sheet than the FIFO method. If costs are falling (an imaginary economy), then inventory purchased more recently cost less than older inventory. In that case, the LIFO method produces a lower Cost of Goods Sold, a higher income, and a higher inventory value on the balance sheet than the FIFO method.

Key Concepts to Remember

1. Inventory is the accounting term for the goods a business holds for sale to its customers in the regular course of business.

2. Beginning inventory is the inventory on hand at the beginning of an accounting period. Ending inventory is the inventory on hand at the end of an accounting period.

3. Cost of Goods Sold is the expense associated with the revenue derived from selling the goods.

4. Cost of Goods Sold = Beginning Inventory + Purchases – Ending Inventory.

5. There are several ways to calculate the cost of goods sold:

   a. Specification identification looks at the cost of the specific goods sold; this is usually used only for high-cost, unique items.

   b. First-in, First-out (FIFO) assumes that goods are sold in the order in which the business originally purchased them. The first units of inventory purchased — the ones the business has held the longest — are assumed to be the first ones sold.

   c. Last-in, First-out (LIFO) assumes that the goods are sold in exactly the opposite of the order in which the business originally purchased them. The units purchased most recently — the ones the business has held the shortest amount of time — are assumed to be the first ones sold.

   d. The average cost method averages the costs of all the units in inventory. To determine the cost of goods sold, you multiply the average cost per unit by the number of units sold.

6. If the replacement cost of a company's inventory is less than its book value, the lower-of-cost-or-market rule may require the company to reduce the balance sheet value of the inventory.

Chapter 11

CONTINGENCIES

"The future you shall know when it has come; before then, forget it."
— *Aeschylus*

THE ACCOUNTING RULES CONCERNING CONTINGENCIES

An interesting[1] accrual problem is what to do about contingencies — losses or gains that may or may not materialize sometime in the future.[2] For example, assume that a customer sues a company in 2014 for $100,000, alleging that a product the company sold the customer is defective. The lawsuit has not yet been tried. This is a ***contingent loss*** to the business — whether the company has to pay the $100,000 depends on the outcome of the litigation. (It is a ***contingent gain*** to the plaintiff — whether the plaintiff receives the $100,000 depends on the outcome of the litigation.) Should this potential liability be accrued and reflected in the company's accounting statements now in spite of its uncertainty or should the company wait until the case is decided?

Accountants are somewhat inconsistent in their treatment of contingent gains and losses, and the inconsistency relates to their gloomy nature, which accountants call the principle of ***conservatism***. As a general rule, accountants believe in painting as negative a picture as possible. Thus, the following rules: Contingent *gains* are never recognized. The customer will not recognize any of the potential gain from the lawsuit until the litigation is concluded. But contingent *losses* must be accrued and reflected on the accounting statements if two conditions are met: (1) it is probable that a loss will occur in the future, and (2) the amount of the loss can be reasonably estimated.[3] If these conditions are met, the company has to include the estimated amount of the loss on its 2014 income statement, even though the case has not yet been decided.

If the company decides that at least one or both of the two conditions is not met — either a contingent loss is not probable or the amount of the loss can't be reasonably estimated — the company does not have to accrue the liability. However, it still has to disclose the contingent liability in a footnote to its financial statements if there is at least a reasonable possibility that a material loss may occur.

---

[1] "Interesting" may be too strong a word. Accountants think it's interesting, but accountants are also mesmerized by the question of whether their socks should match their pants or their shirt.

[2] Income from the future sales of this book is a contingency for the author, although an extremely remote one.

[3] Financial Accounting Standards Board, Accounting Standards Codification § 450-25-2.

ACCRUING CONTINGENCIES

If the loss contingency is accrued and recognized, the probable amount of the loss is treated as a current expense and charged against income for the period. The offsetting entry to make the accounts balance is to create a liability with a name like Contingent Liability. Thus, if the company believes that it will lose the lawsuit and its estimated damages are $85,000, it will include an $85,000 Litigation Expense on its income statement and show an $85,000 liability with a name like Contingent Litigation Liability on its balance sheet. The journal entry would look like this:

Litigation Expense	$85,000	
Contingent Litigation Liability		$85,000

If the contingency eventually occurs (the company loses the lawsuit), the contingent liability account is eliminated and the Cash account reduced by the amount paid. If the company gets lucky and the contingency does not occur (the company wins the lawsuit), the contingent liability account is still eliminated. The offsetting entry is to reduce the expense for the current period, to make up for the amount that was previously charged against income but never incurred.

GROUPS OF RELATED CONTINGENCIES

A company sometimes faces a group of related contingencies. A company that sells its products on credit has many accounts receivable, some of which may not be paid. A company that sells consumer products may face a large number of warranty or product defect claims, only some of which it will lose.

The company may not know whether *any particular one* of those individual claims will succeed, but it may be able to estimate, based on past experience, that a certain percentage of all the warranty claims will be successful or that a certain percentage of all the accounts receivable will be uncollectible. Considering each individual claim alone, the two-part test for recognizing a loss contingency is not met. The company cannot say whether a loss is probable. However, considering all of the claims as a group, the company can say that a loss is probable and can reasonably estimate its amount, because it can estimate the overall percentage of claims that will succeed.

If this is the case, the company must accrue the expected amount of the loss on a group basis, in the same way that it would accrue an individual loss contingency. In the accounts receivable example, it would add the probable amount of the loss to an account called something like Allowance for Uncollectible Accounts and the offsetting entry would be an Uncollectible Accounts Expense that appears on the income statement.

It is customary to show the Allowance for Uncollectible Accounts as an offset to Accounts Receivable on the asset side of the balance sheet. For example, if the company has Accounts Receivable of $150,000 and estimates that 10% of that amount is uncollectible, that portion of the assets section of the balance sheet would look like this:

| Accounts Receivable | $150,000 | |
| Less: Allowance for Uncollectible Accounts | (15,000) | $135,000 |

"RESERVE" ACCOUNTS AND THE VOLUNTARY TREATMENT OF CONTINGENCIES

Even if a company is not required to accrue a contingent loss and treat it as a current expense, it may still want to show the contingency on its balance sheet. This is sometimes done by creating a "reserve" account in the equity section of the balance sheet.

Recall that the equity or net worth section of the balance sheet represents the net worth of the business — the residual difference between assets and liabilities. If a contingency materializes, it will reduce equity. It is therefore customary to record such a reserve account separately in the equity section of the balance sheet, indicating that there is no liability yet but, if the contingency occurs, the equity of the business will be reduced by the amount of the reserve.

This account is usually called something like Provision for Contingency or Reserve for Contingency. The use of the term "reserve" is disfavored because it falsely implies that money has been set aside to pay the contingency. That is not the case. The creation of this account is only an accounting entry.

If the contingency materializes and the business suffers a loss, the reserve account is eliminated and the loss is charged against net income as an expense. If the contingency does not eventually materialize, the reserve account is eliminated.

Key Concepts to Remember

1. A contingency is a loss or gain that has not yet occurred, but may occur at some point in the future.

2. Accountants believe in conservatism, so they do not recognize contingent gains until they actually occur.

3. Loss contingencies must be accrued and reflected on the accounting statements if two conditions are met: (1) it is probable that the loss will occur in the future and (2) the amount of the loss can be reasonably estimated.

4. If a loss contingency does not meet those requirements, but there is at least a reasonable possibility it will occur, the contingency must still be disclosed in the footnotes to the financial statements.

5. Companies sometimes use "reserve" accounts in the equity section of their balance sheets to reflect a contingency that has not been accrued. The creation of this account does not mean that any money has been set aside to pay the contingency.

Chapter 12

CASH FLOW: THE STATEMENT OF CASH FLOWS

"There is nothing quite as wonderful as money.
There is nothing quite as beautiful as cash.
Some people say it's folly,
But I'd rather have the lolly.
With money you can make a splash."
— *Eric Idle and John Gould*

In 2012, Boston Scientific had an annual net loss of more than $4 billion; it had lost over a billion dollars each year in three of the four years prior to that.[1] Yet Boston Scientific remained in business. Boston Scientific is not alone; other companies have had large operating losses for several consecutive years and still continued to operate. On the other hand, many companies with consistently good incomes have difficulty continuing in business. For example, in 1989, Prime Motor Inns, at the time the second largest hotel operator in the world, had revenues of $410 million and a net income of $77 million. In spite of this impressive showing, Prime Motor Inns filed for bankruptcy.[2]

What explains this discrepancy between a company's income or losses and its ability to remain in business? The answer lies, at least in part, in **cash flows**. Boston Scientific and other companies which continue in business despite massive losses either have sufficient cash reserves (savings) to weather the problems or they can obtain cash by selling assets, selling stock, or borrowing money. Companies like Prime Motor Inns may be profitable, but their profits are tied up in assets other than cash. Unfortunately, you can't pay creditors and employees with buildings, equipment, or inventory. Without cash to pay bills, a company can be forced into bankruptcy.

The experiences of many law students also illustrate why cash flows, and not just net income, are important. During law school, you are probably operating at a net loss. Your expenses — what you're paying for food, rent, tuition, and so forth — are greater than your income from your work and any investments you might have. You are able to continue in law school only because you have additional cash available — loans, scholarships, or savings from past work. Even though you have a net operating loss, you have sufficient cash (barely) to pay your bills.

---

[1] These numbers are taken from the financial statements included in Boston Scientific's annual reports to shareholders. Boston Scientific's annual reports, as well as the annual reports of any other U.S. public company, are available on the SEC's web site at http://www.sec.gov/edgar/searchedgar/companysearch.html.

[2] Dana Linden, *Lies of the Bottom Line*, FORBES, Nov. 12, 1990, at 106.

Let's consider your **cash flow** — where your cash comes from and where it goes. A list of your sources of cash would probably look something like this:

- Money from a part-time job
- Student loans
- Loans from parents
- Grants from government agencies
- Scholarships
- Gifts from parents, grandparents, and others
- Sales of assets you own, such as your car, your furniture, blood plasma, and body parts.[3]

A list of how you spend your cash might look like this:

- Rent and other bills
- Food and entertainment[4]
- Tuition
- Books
- Taxes
- Interest
- Repayment of loans
- Automobile
- Bribes to professors for good grades.[5]

You may have other sources of cash and you may spend your cash in other ways, but these lists are fairly typical. The net difference between the cash coming in and the cash going out is known as your **net cash flow**. If you're taking in more cash than you're spending, your net cash flow is positive. If you're spending more cash than you're taking in, your net cash flow is negative.

Businesses receive and disburse cash in much the same ways and for similar purposes[6] as law students. A company's cash flows are usually grouped into three categories: (1) cash flows from operating activities; (2) cash flows from investing activities; and (3) cash flows from financing activities. A company's **operating activities** are the transactions associated with its sales of goods and services — cash received from sales and the cash paid for expenses to produce those sales. Cash flow from operating activities also includes interest paid on loans the company makes to others and dividends received from stock in other companies. A company's **cash flow**

---

[3] "I'd give an arm and a leg to go to law school."

[4] Yes, let's call that big party last weekend from which you're still recovering "entertainment."

[5] To my students: This last item is only a joke, of course. (Forward any cash to Account No. 51C37S4 at the National Bank of Costa Rica.)

[6] That's "purposes," not "porpoises." Very few businesses, although a surprising number of law students, spend cash for porpoises.

from investing activities includes payments to acquire property, plant, and equipment, to make loans, and to make equity investments in other companies. It also includes cash received from selling those assets and investments, and to repay the principal on those loans made to others. A company's **cash flow from financing activities** relate to its liabilities and equity accounts — the cash received by borrowing money and paid out to repay those loans, the cash received from investors (as when a corporation sells stock), and the cash paid out to investors (as when a corporation pays dividends to its stockholders or repurchases its stock). What goes into each category is somewhat arbitrary; some of the items might easily have been put into another category, but this is how the accounting rules split it up.

THE STATEMENT OF CASH FLOWS

The **Statement of Cash Flows** is an accounting statement that tracks a company's or individual's cash flow for a specified period. It shows how much cash the company had at the start of the period, the amount of cash it received during the period, the amount of cash it paid out during the period, and how much cash the company had at the end of the period. The relationship between these different amounts is fairly simple:

$$\text{Cash, Beginning of Period} + \text{Cash Coming In} - \text{Cash Going Out} = \text{Cash, End of Period}$$

The Statement of Cash Flows may be prepared in one of two ways: the **Direct Method** or the **Indirect Method**.[7] The difference between them is in how they determine cash flows from operations. Cash flows from investing activities and cash flows from financing activities are the same under both methods.

The **Direct Method** looks to each of the various accounts and asks how much cash was paid or received in connection with each account during the period. How much of the company's revenues were received in cash in the period? How much cash did the company pay for various expenses during the period?

The **Indirect Method**, which almost all big businesses use, begins with net income for the period as a starting point. Net income is not the same as cash flow because of the accrual method of accounting. Recall that, under the accrual method, revenues and expenses may be recognized before or after cash is transferred. To convert net income to cash flow, we have to reverse all the accruals and deferrals and get back to the cash basis of accounting.

For instance, assume that a company has Total Revenues for the year of $300,000 and Total Expenses of $250,000, giving it a Net Income of $50,000. Assume that all revenues were received in cash, so no adjustments need to be made to revenues. But one of the expenses was depreciation, in the amount of $5,000. Depreciation expense reduced the company's net income by $5,000, but no cash is paid out for depreciation. It's merely a bookkeeping entry. The company's net cash flow was actually $5,000

---

[7] The names of the methods are boring, but what do you expect from accountants?

greater than its net income, so we have to add the $5,000 back in to determine the company's net cash flow, $55,000.

Here's a more detailed example. Assume that Acme Corporation's balance sheets for 2013 and 2014 look like this:

Acme Corporation
Balance Sheets
As of December 31, 2013 and 2014

2013

Assets			*Liabilities and Shareholders' Equity*	
Cash	$4,600		Liabilities	
Inventory	500		Accounts Payable	$600
			Long-Term Debt	500
			Shareholders' Equity	4,000
Total Assets	$5,100		Total Liabilities and Shareholders' Equity	$5,100

2014

Assets			*Liabilities and Shareholders' Equity*	
Cash		$5,000	Liabilities	
Inventory		600	Accounts Payable	$800
Equipment	$2,500		Long-Term Debt	0
Less: Accum. Depr.	500	2,000	Shareholders' Equity	6,800
Total Assets		$7,600	Total Liabilities and Shareholders' Equity	$7,600

The company's income statement for 2014 looks like this:

Acme Corporation
Income Statement
For the Year Ended December 31, 2014

Sales Revenue		$ 46,000
Expenses:		
Wages	$ 32,000	
Cost of Goods Sold	5,200	
Depreciation	500	
Total Expenses		37,700
Net Income		$ 8,300

Acme's net cash flow during 2014 is obvious from the two balance sheets. All you have to do is compare the Cash accounts. At the end of 2013, Acme had $4,600 cash. At the end of 2014, it had $5,000 cash, $400 more. Its net cash flow during 2014 was an increase of $400. Let's prepare a Statement of Cash Flows to see why, with a net income of $8,300 in 2014, Acme's cash only increased by $400:

Acme Corporation
Statement of Cash Flows
2014

Cash Flows From Operating Activities		
Net Income	$ 8,300	
Adjustments to reconcile net income		
to cash provided by operations:		
Increase in Inventory	(100)	
Increase in Accounts Payable	200	
Depreciation Expense	500	
Cash Provided by Operating Activities		$8,900
Cash Flows From Investing Activities		
Purchase of Equipment		(2,500)
Cash Flows From Financing Activities		
Retirement of long-term debt	$ (500)	
Sale of Stock	1,000	
Payment of Dividends	(6,500)	
Total Cash Flows From Financing Activities		(6,000)
Total Increase in Cash		$400
Cash, December 31, 2013		4,600
Cash, December 31, 2014		$5,000

Using the indirect method, we start with the company's net income, $8,300. We must subtract all the cash payments the company made that were not treated as current expenses and therefore did not affect net income. We must add back all of the cash receipts the company had that were not treated as revenues and therefore did not affect net income. We must reverse any expenses or revenues that were accrued, where no cash has yet changed hands. And we must include any expenses or revenues that were deferred, where cash has been paid, but not yet charged to income. What's left after we make all of these adjustments should be the company's net cash flow.

Cash from Operations increased not just by the $8,300 of net income but by $8,900. Three adjustments to Net Income are necessary. First, the company increased its Inventory, using cash to purchase a non-cash asset which didn't affect net income. Second, the company delayed paying some legitimate debts (Accounts Payable) and saved the cash, even though the debts were treated as expenses to calculate net income. Third, the company had an expense (Depreciation) for which no cash was paid.

Look now at cash flows from investing activities. The company used $2,500 of its cash to purchase new equipment, which is an investing activity. Except for the $500 that was depreciated in 2014, this is not an expense, so it did not reduce net income.

Turn now to financing activities. Five hundred dollars of the remaining difference is due to the retirement of debt — the company used $500 cash to pay off its long-term debt. The company sold stock for $1,000, increasing its cash by $1,000. And it paid cash dividends of $6,500, reducing its cash by $6,500.

When we add and subtract all of these adjustments, the company's net cash flow is a $400 gain, the difference between the Cash accounts on the two balance sheets.

Key Concepts to Remember

1. Cash flow is a company's use and receipt of cash.

2. The Statement of Cash Flows is an accounting statement that tracks a company's cash flow over a specified period of time. It explains the difference between the cash balance on the balance sheet at the beginning of the period and the cash balance on the balance sheet at the end of the period.

3. The Statement of Cash Flows is divided into three sections, showing cash flow from operating activities, investing activities, and financing activities.

4. There are two ways to calculate cash flow from operating activities, the direct method and the indirect method. Most companies use the indirect method, which starts with net income for the period, adds back in cash flows that did not affect income, and eliminates non-cash items that do affect income.

Section Four

THE ACCOUNTING ENVIRONMENT

Chapter 13

INTRODUCTION TO THE ACCOUNTING ENVIRONMENT

"There's no business like show business, but there are several businesses like accounting."
— *David Letterman*

Public companies in the United States are required to prepare financial statements — the balance sheet, income statement, statement of cash flows, and statement of changes in equity that you read about in earlier chapters — and file those financial statements with the Securities and Exchange Commission (SEC). They must also include those financial statements in the annual reports they are required to send to shareholders.

Those financial statements are prepared by the company itself, not by any independent outsider. However, the financial statements must be prepared in accordance with generally accepted accounting principles, discussed in Chapter 14. In addition, the financial statements of U.S. public companies must be audited — reviewed by an independent accounting firm known as an auditor. That audit must be conducted in accordance with generally accepted auditing standards. We will discuss auditors and auditing in Chapter 16.

Public companies' financial statements and the audit opinions accompanying them, as well as a wealth of other information about those companies, are publicly available. You can find them on the SEC's web site, www.sec.gov.

Not all companies are subject to these requirements. Smaller companies are not required to prepare financial statements. They often do, but those financial statements may not be publicly available. And there is no general requirement that those non-public companies' financial statements be audited. However, many non-public companies have their financial statements audited even though they are not required by law to do so.

Key Concepts to Remember

1. U.S. public companies must prepare financial statements in accordance with generally accepted accounting principles. Those financial statements are reviewed by outside auditors in accordance with generally accepted auditing standards.

2. Public companies' financial statements are filed with the SEC and are publicly available.

3. Most smaller, non-public companies do not have to comply with these requirements. However, even non-public companies may prepare audited financial statements.

Chapter 14

GENERALLY ACCEPTED ACCOUNTING PRINCIPLES

'I worked as an accountant for a number of years in Chicago and I had a kind of strange theory of accountancy. I always felt that, if you got within two or three bucks of it . . . But this never really caught on."
— Bob Newhart

INTRODUCTION

This book is an introduction to basic accounting principles, but where do those rules come from and how do accountants know what they are? What keeps accountants from just making up numbers?

Accountants prepare financial statements and accounting records in accordance with what are known as ***generally accepted accounting principles***, commonly abbreviated as ***GAAP***.[1] But who controls what is accepted and what is not?

The answer to that question lies in a confusing morass of governmental, quasi-governmental, and private regulation. The primary governmental regulator is the ***Securities and Exchange Commission***, or ***SEC***, a five-person commission whose members are appointed by the President. The primary private regulator is the ***Financial Accounting Standards Board***, or ***FASB***.[2] The third major player is the ***Public Company Accounting Oversight Board***, or ***PCAOB***, which is best described as a quasi-private, quasi-governmental hybrid. The PCAOB's primary focus is on auditors and the auditing process, which we will discuss in greater detail in Chapter 16. In this chapter, we will focus on the SEC and the FASB.

THE FINANCIAL ACCOUNTING STANDARDS BOARD (FASB)

The leading source of GAAP in the United States is the Financial Accounting Standards Board, a private, independent body with seven full-time members.[3] The SEC, pursuant to authority granted by the Sarbanes-Oxley Act of 2002,[4] has

---

[1] This acronym is pronounced "gap," like the jeans store and the space between David Letterman's front teeth.

[2] This is pronounced faz bee.

[3] The FASB has a counterpart, the Governmental Accounting Standards Board (GASB), which establishes accounting principles for state and local governments. I briefly discuss the GASB and governmental accounting in Chapter 19.

[4] *See* Securities Act of 1933 § 19(b), 15 U.S.C. § 77s(b).

designated the FASB as an authoritative source of generally accepted accounting principles for purposes of the federal securities laws.[5] But the SEC accepted the FASB as a source of GAAP long before the Sarbanes-Oxley Act was passed. Since 1938, the SEC has indicated that financial statements that were inconsistent with the standards promulgated by the FASB (and its predecessors) were presumed to be misleading.[6] That essentially gave accountants and their clients a choice between following the FASB rules or committing federal securities fraud.

The SEC's designation of the FASB as standard-setter only applies to companies subject to federal securities regulation, primarily large, publicly traded companies. But the rules governing auditors prohibit auditors from opining that financial statements are in accord with generally accepted accounting principles if those statements depart from the FASB principles in a material way. As a result, the FASB's rules essentially establish GAAP for all U.S. companies.

In 2009, the FASB codified U.S. GAAP into the *FASB Accounting Standards Codification*.[7] Changes to those standards are announced in *Accounting Standards Updates*. Prior to 2009, accounting pronouncements from the FASB and its staff came in a number of different forms: (1) *Statements of Financial Accounting Standards (SFAS)*; (2) *Interpretations*; (3) *Statements of Financial Accounting Concepts*; and (4) *Technical Bulletins*.[8] The Codification supersedes all of those earlier pronouncements.

THE SECURITIES AND EXCHANGE COMMISSION (SEC)

The SEC has the authority to directly prescribe accounting principles for financial statements filed pursuant to the federal securities laws.[9] The SEC has, for the most part, deferred to the FASB and its predecessors, but the SEC does have its own accounting regulations and releases.

Regulation S-X is the SEC's principal accounting regulation, and the SEC also issues releases dealing with accounting issues. *Financial Reporting Releases (FRRs)*, the most important, are official statements by the SEC of accounting policies and standards. Before 1982, these releases were known as *Accounting Series Releases (ASRs)*; in 1982, the SEC incorporated all of the ASRs into Financial Reporting Release No. 1. The SEC staff also issues its own *Staff Accounting Bulletins*, informal statements of interpretations and practices the staff follows. Other

---

[5] Commission Statement of Policy Reaffirming the Status of the FASB as a Designated Private-Sector Standard Setter, Securities Act Release No. 8221 (Apr. 25, 2003).

[6] Accounting Series Release No. 4; Financial Reporting Release No. 1 § 101.

[7] The FASB codification is available online. *See* Financial Accounting Standards Board, Accounting Standards Codification, https://asc.fasb.org/. You can access the basic view for free after a quick registration.

[8] Prior to the creation of the FASB in 1972, authoritative statements on accounting principles were published by two entities affiliated with the *American Institute of Certified Public Accountants (AICPA)*: the AICPA *Committee on Accounting Procedure (CAP)* from 1938 to 1959; and the *Accounting Principles Board (APB)* from 1959 to 1972.

[9] Securities Act of 1933 § 19(a), 15 U.S.C. § 77s(a); Securities Exchange Act of 1934 § 13(b)(1), 15 U.S.C. § 78m(b)(1).

SEC releases and regulations touch on accounting issues in many different contexts.

THE INTERNAL REVENUE CODE

The Internal Revenue Code and the corresponding Treasury regulations often specify their own, unique accounting rules to be used in computing federal tax liabilities. As a result, the calculations a company does for tax purposes may differ substantially from how the company prepares its financial statements. For tax purposes, companies look to the requirements in the Internal Revenue Code and Treasury regulations.

INTERNATIONAL ISSUES

The standard-setting picture is complicated further when one looks beyond the United States. The SEC, the FASB, and the PCAOB are all U.S. entities. They regulate U.S. accounting practices, but their jurisdiction to set accounting principles does not extend beyond our borders.

Generally accepted accounting principles often vary substantially from country to country. For example, Daimler-Benz, a German company, had a $1 billion loss one year under U.S. GAAP, but a $100 million profit when the same data were compiled using German accounting principles.[10]

There is a push toward international uniformity, led by the *International Accounting Standards Board*, or *IASB*. Its standards are known as *International Financial Reporting Standards (IFRS)*. The United States participates in IASB standard-setting, but has not fully adopted the international standards. In 2007, the SEC decided to accept financial statements prepared by *foreign* companies in accordance with IFRS issued by the IASB. Prior to that, the SEC had required foreign companies to reconcile their financial statements to U.S. GAAP. At one time, the SEC was moving towards the adoption of IFRS to replace the current U.S. GAAP, even for U.S. companies. But that movement towards international convergence has slowed considerably and it's not clear when or if it will happen.

The rules in this book are pretty basic; most, but certainly not all, of them would be the same no matter the jurisdiction. To keep it simple, we'll focus on U.S. GAAP.[11]

---

[10] Lee Berton, *All Accountants Soon May Speak the Same Language*, WALL ST. J., Aug. 29, 1995, at A15.

[11] The fact that I'm less familiar with the international rules has nothing to do with it. (Really!)

Key Concepts to Remember

1. Accountants prepare financial statements and accounting records in accordance with what are known as generally accepted accounting principles, commonly abbreviated as GAAP.

2. The leading source of GAAP in the United States is the Financial Accounting Standards Board (FASB), a private body. The FASB has been designated as an authoritative source of generally accepted accounting principles by the Securities and Exchange Commission (SEC). Even when the SEC rules don't apply, certified public accountants are generally required to follow the FASB rules.

3. The FASB publishes an authoritative codification of generally accepted accounting principles.

4. The SEC has, for the most part, deferred to the FASB, but it also has its own accounting rules applicable to companies required to file reports with the SEC.

5. Tax accounting rules sometimes differ from GAAP.

6. Other countries have their own accounting rules. The International Accounting Standards Board (IASB) is the leading international standard-setter.

Chapter 15

NOTES TO THE FINANCIAL STATEMENTS; MD&A

"Nobody was ever meant
To remember or invent
What he did with every cent."
— Robert Frost

At the end of every company's financial statements, you will find a section with a name like ***Notes to Financial Statements***. The Notes section usually covers several pages and is often quite complex.

The notes to the financial statements are as important as the financial statements themselves, so don't skip them. They are not like the footnotes in law reviews, whose sole function is to put you to sleep. The notes to the financial statements are vital to understanding the numbers in the financial statements and how they were generated.[1]

Much of the content of the notes is required, either by GAAP or by SEC rules. Even if a particular explanatory note is not expressly required, it may be necessary to keep the financial statements from being misleading and exposing the company to liability for fraud. A company may also voluntarily include in the notes additional information it believes is necessary to provide a fair picture of the company's business or operations. The additional information in the notes allows the company to "make its case" to investors and other users of the financial statements.

DISCLOSURE OF ACCOUNTING PRINCIPLES

Companies are required by GAAP to explain the accounting principles, practices, and methods they used to prepare the financial statements — how they came up with the particular numbers. This explanation usually appears at the first of the notes section. The explanation of the company's accounting practices is particularly important where two or more alternative principles or approaches are acceptable under GAAP — for example, the choice among depreciation methods or different ways of valuing inventory.

Changes in the company's accounting methods must also be reported. The financial statements usually report results for more than one period to allow a comparison of the present statements with those from prior years. The same accounting principles must usually be followed period after period, but changes from one method to another are permitted in certain circumstances. For example, a company may sometimes change the way it values inventory. A change of accounting methods makes it difficult

---

[1] They're also pretty good at putting you to sleep.

to compare the current period to prior periods. Any change of this sort must be disclosed in the notes and, to make comparisons easier, the notes will often restate the financial statements from the prior period using the new accounting method.

EVENTS NOT REFLECTED IN THE FINANCIAL STATEMENTS

The footnotes may also contain information about events or transactions that are not reflected in the financial statements. For example, a company may use the footnotes to describe a future contingency or commitment that is not accrued as an expense. If, for example, material litigation is pending against the company, the company can describe the litigation and the likelihood of success. Even if the contingency has been accrued on the financial statements, a note might still be necessary to provide additional detail.

The company can also use the notes to describe any significant events that occurred after the balance sheet and the income statement were prepared. For example, if the company's balance sheet shows assets and liabilities as of December 31 and the company's warehouse exploded on January 2, a footnote disclosing this subsequent event can avoid misleading anyone.

OTHER SUPPLEMENTAL INFORMATION

The company can also use the footnotes to provide greater detail, including non-quantitative data,[2] about items that are reported on the financial statements. It is common, for example, for companies to include a note providing additional detail about the stockholder's equity accounts: descriptions of the different classes of stock and their rights, descriptions of what produced any changes in the equity accounts, and descriptions of any outstanding stock options or rights that are not currently reflected in the equity accounts but might affect them in the future. As another example, if the company has been involved in a significant merger or acquisition, the company might explain how it accounted for the transaction and what effect the transaction had on the financial statements, so the effect of the acquisition on the financial statements can be separated from the effect of the company's regular operations.

MANAGEMENT'S DISCUSSION AND ANALYSIS (MD&A)

Another source of important financial information is worth mentioning, even though it's not in the financial statements or the notes to the financial statements. The SEC requires public companies to include in their annual reports a section called *Management's Discussion and Analysis of Financial Condition and Results of Operations*, typically called just *Management's Discussion and Analysis* or *MD&A* for short. This section is intended to provide a narrative explanation of the financial statements, including "known trends, demands, commitments, events, or uncertainties" that are reasonably likely to result in material changes in the company's liquidity, capital

---

[2] For those of you who still haven't mastered accounting jargon, this would be what lay people call text.

resources, sales, revenues, or income in the future.[3] The MD&A section must also discuss off-balance sheet arrangements that are likely to affect the company's finances in a material way.[4] It's always wise to look at the Management's Discussion and Analysis to see if it flags anything important financially that might not be apparent from the financial statements and the notes to the financial statements.

Key Concepts to Remember

1. You should pay careful attention to the notes accompanying financial statements. They are as important as the statements themselves.

2. The notes disclose the accounting methods the company uses, disclose important events not reflected in the financial statements, and provide a variety of other useful, supplemental information.

3. Another useful source of information for public companies is the Management's Discussion and Analysis (MD&A) section of those companies' annual reports.

---

[3] The full requirements are in Item 303 of the SEC's Regulation S-K, 17 C.F.R. § 229.303 (2011).

[4] Item 303(a)(4), Regulation S-K, 17 C.F.R. § 229.303(a)(4) (2011).

Chapter 16

AUDITING

"It's fun to charter an accountant
And sail the wide accountancy
To find, explore the funds offshore
And skirt the shoals of bankruptcy."
— Eric Idle and John Du Prez

Publicly-owned companies (and some other companies) in the United States have their financial statements *audited.* An *auditor* is an independent, outside accountant who examines the company's accounting system to determine the reliability of the company's financial statements. A company may have its own *internal auditors*, company employees who monitor the company's accounting controls and report problems to management. But the more important audit for publicly-owned companies is the independent audit conducted by *certified public accountants (CPAs).*

Companies, or accountants under their control, prepare their own financial statements; they are not prepared by outsiders. The purpose of the audit is to provide an outside check on the numbers the company has prepared internally. The CPAs who do these audits are not employees of the company; they are independent outside accountants hired by the company to examine the company's accounting statements and opine on their accuracy.

Auditors issue *audit opinions* that indicate, among other things, whether the company's financial statements were prepared in accordance with generally accepted accounting principles (GAAP). These audit opinions appear with the company's financial statements and are relied on by outsiders such as lenders and investors.

THE REGULATION OF AUDITORS AND THE AUDITING PROCESS

Audits must be conducted in accordance with *generally accepted auditing standards (GAAS)*. Until 2002, auditing in the United States was regulated primarily by the *Auditing Standards Board (ASB)*, a committee of the American Institute of Certified Public Accountants (AICPA). The AICPA is the private professional association of CPAs, the accounting equivalent of the American Bar Association.

In 2002, the Sarbanes-Oxley Act created the *Public Company Accounting Oversight Board (PCAOB)*. The PCAOB has the power, subject to SEC oversight, to set auditing and ethics standards for accounting firms that audit public companies. The PCAOB also reviews and disciplines those accounting firms. The ASB continues to exist; it just no longer has jurisdiction over the auditing of public companies.

One of the PCAOB's first actions was to adopt the existing standards of the AICPA. However, since then, the PCAOB has been enacting its own standards and the AICPA standards have changed. Therefore, the PCAOB audit standards, applicable to the audits of public companies, and the ASB audit standards, applicable to all other audits, now differ, although not in a major way. Both sets of standards are publicly available.[1]

Among other things, the auditing standards are designed to assure that the auditor is sufficiently independent of the audited company so that conflicts of interest do not affect the auditor's work. The point of the audit, after all, is to provide an *independent* check on the financial statements prepared by the company's management.

THE AUDIT REPORT

When the audit is completed, the auditor issues an audit report. The audit report describes the financial statements the auditor reviewed and explains that the financial statements are the responsibility of the company's management. In the case of a public company, the audit report must specifically indicate that the audit was done in accordance with standards established by the PCAOB, and briefly describe what the audit process entails. And, if the company is required by the Sarbanes-Oxley Act to obtain an auditor's report on the effectiveness of its internal controls,[2] the audit report must include a paragraph referring to the internal controls report.

If the auditor finds no material problem, the opinion will be *clean* or *unqualified*. An unqualified opinion says that the financial statements fairly present the company's financial position in conformity with generally accepted accounting principles. If the auditor finds a material problem with the financial statements, the opinion will be *qualified* or *adverse*. The difference between a qualified opinion and an adverse opinion is one of degree. A qualified opinion indicates that there is some limited problem with the financial statements, but the financial statements otherwise fairly present the company's financial position. An adverse opinion indicates that, taken as a whole, the financial statements do not fairly present the company's financial position in accordance with GAAP.

An unqualified audit opinion for a public company will look like this[3]:

Report of Independent Registered Public Accounting Firm

To the Board of Directors and Stockholders of X Corporation:

We have audited the accompanying balance sheets of X Corporation as of December 31, 2013 and 2012, and the related statements of operations, comprehensive income, stockholders' equity, and cash flows for each of the

---

[1] *See* http://pcaob.org/Standards/Auditing (PCAOB standards); Audit and Attest Standards, Including Clarified Standards, http://www.aicpa.org/RESEARCH/STANDARDS/AUDITATTEST/Pages/audit%20and%20attest%20standards.aspx (AICPA standards).

[2] I discuss the internal controls report in Chapter 18.

[3] This opinion is based on the PCAOB standards; an audit of a non-public company under the AICPA standards would look slightly different. As this book went to press, the PCAOB had proposed, but not adopted, revisions to the audit standards that would add additional content to the audit report.

three years in the period ended December 31, 2013. These financial statements are the responsibility of the company's management. Our responsibility is to express an opinion on these financial statements based on our audits.

We conducted our audits in accordance with the standards of the Public Company Accounting Oversight Board (United States). Those standards require that we plan and perform the audit to obtain reasonable assurance about whether the financial statements are free of material misstatement. An audit also includes examining, on a test basis, evidence supporting the amounts and disclosures in the financial statements. An audit also includes assessing the accounting principles used and significant estimates made by management, as well as evaluating the overall financial statement presentation. We believe that our audits provide a reasonable basis for our opinion.

In our opinion, the financial statements referred to above present fairly, in all material respects, the financial position of X Corporation as of December 31, 2013 and 2012, and the results of its operations and its cash flows for each of the three years in the period ended December 31, 2013, in conformity with U.S. generally accepted accounting principles.

We have also audited, in accordance with the standards of the Public Company Accounting Oversight Board (United States), X Corporation's internal control over financial reporting as of December 31, 2013, based on criteria established in *Internal Control — Integrated Framework* issued by the Committee of Sponsoring Organizations of the Treadway Commission (COSO) and our report dated January 30, 2014 expressed an unqualified opinion thereon.

/s/ Dense & Obtuse
Certified Public Accountants
January 30, 2014

Look carefully at the third paragraph. This opinion is the auditor's version of a clean bill of health. Applying generally accepted auditing standards, the auditor found nothing materially wrong. If you see exceptions or qualifications — anything other than this basic language — you need to pay careful attention.

Key Concepts to Remember

1. Most publicly-owned companies and some other companies have their financial statements audited. An auditor is an independent, outside accountant who examines the company's accounting system to determine the reliability of the company's financial statements.

2. Audits must be conducted in accordance with generally accepted auditing standards (GAAS). In the United States, the audits of public companies are regulated by the Public Company Accounting Oversight Board (PCAOB). Auditing standards for non-public companies are established by the Auditing Standards Board (ASB), a committee of the American Institute of Certified Public Accountants (AICPA).

3. The audit opinion appears with the company's financial statements. If the auditor finds a material problem with the financial statements, the opinion will be either qualified or adverse. If the auditor finds no material problem, the auditor will issue a clean, or unqualified, opinion.

Chapter 17

LAWYERS' RESPONSES TO AUDIT INQUIRIES

"A man may as well open an oyster without a knife as a lawyer's mouth without a fee."

— Barten Holyday

In Chapter 11, you learned that companies are sometimes required to accrue or disclose contingent liabilities — possible future liabilities that the company has not yet had to pay.[1] One thing auditors need to review is whether the company has properly reflected its contingent liabilities in the financial statements. As part of that review, the auditor asks the audited company to provide it with information about legal claims against the company, both claims that have already been asserted (such as pending litigation) and claims that could be asserted in the future. The auditor also requires the company to send a letter to its outside attorneys asking them to provide the auditor with information about those claims. This letter is known as an ***audit inquiry letter***.

This request to the lawyer poses a tension between the auditor's need for information and the confidentiality of the attorney-client relationship. The accounting and legal professions have entered into a "treaty" designed to accommodate both professions' interests. The attorney's side of that treaty is reflected in the American Bar Association's *Statement of Policy Regarding Lawyers' Responses to Auditors' Requests for Information*.[2] U.S. attorneys follow that *Statement of Policy* in responding to the auditor.

The *Statement of Policy* has three major elements: (1) a requirement that the client consent to the lawyer's disclosure to the auditor; (2) limits on the matters the lawyer may comment on; and (3) limits on what the lawyer may say about those matters.

CLIENT CONSENT

The lawyer may not provide information to the outside auditor without the client's consent. In most cases, the client's request to the lawyer in the audit inquiry letter is sufficient consent. However, if the lawyer's response will disclose confidences or evaluate a claim, the audit inquiry letter is not itself sufficient consent. The lawyer must get the client's informed consent, after the lawyer provides "full disclosure to the client of the legal consequences of such action."[3] The most important legal consequences are the possibilities that the lawyer's response will waive the attorney-client

---

[1] If you didn't learn that, go back to Chapter 11. I expect you to memorize everything in this book.

[2] American Bar Association, *Statement of Policy Regarding Lawyers' Responses to Auditors' Requests for Information*, 31 Bus. Law. 1709 (1976).

[3] *Id.*, at 1711.

privilege or will constitute an admission that could be used against the client in the future.

THE MATTERS LAWYERS MAY COMMENT ON

Attorneys may provide information about three types of loss contingencies: (1) overtly threatened or pending litigation; (2) contractually assumed obligations; and (3) unasserted possible claims or assessments. However, the attorney may comment on the last two items only if the client has specifically identified them in the audit inquiry letter and requested comment.[4]

WHAT THE LAWYER MAY SAY ABOUT THOSE MATTERS

Basic Information. In all cases, the lawyer may provide basic information about the legal contingencies: "an identification of the proceedings or matter, the stage of proceedings, the claim(s) asserted, and the position taken by the client."[5] If certain conditions are met, the lawyer may provide two more types of information: (1) a judgment as to the probable outcome of the case; and (2) an estimate of the probable amount of any loss.

Prediction of the Outcome. The lawyer may express a judgment as to the possible outcome of the matter only if the likelihood of an outcome unfavorable to the client — for instance, the likelihood that the client will lose a lawsuit — is "probable" or "remote." A loss is probable if the client has only a "slight" chance of *winning* and it is "extremely doubtful" that the other side will lose. A loss is remote if the client has only a "slight" chance of *losing* and it is "extremely doubtful" that the other side will win. If, as in most cases, the likelihood of an unfavorable outcome falls between those two extremes, the lawyer may not comment on the outcome.

Amount of the Possible Loss. The lawyer may estimate the potential amount of a loss or range of loss only if she believes the probability that her estimate will be inaccurate is slight.[6] If this standard is met, the lawyer may, for example, say that the amount of the loss if the client loses will be "between $50,000 and $100,000."

---

[4] The client is supposed to ask the lawyer to comment on unasserted possible claims "only if the client has determined that it is probable that a possible claim will be asserted, that there is a reasonable possibility that the outcome (assuming such assertion) will be unfavorable, and that the resulting liability would be material to the financial condition of the client." *Id.*, at 1712.

[5] *Id.*, at 1713.

[6] In any event, the lawyer may not provide such an estimate if the possibility of an unfavorable outcome is "remote."

Key Concepts to Remember

1. To facilitate the audits of their financial statements, companies send audit inquiry letters to their outside counsel asking them to comment on legal contingencies.

2. Lawyers respond to those audit inquiries in accordance with the American Bar Association's *Statement of Policy*. The Statement of Policy requires the client to consent to any disclosure; sometimes "informed consent" is required.

3. If the client consents to disclosure, the lawyer may comment on overtly threatened and pending litigation and, if the client specifically requests comment, contractually assumed obligations, and unasserted claims.

4. The lawyer may provide basic information about the legal contingency and the client's position. In certain, limited circumstances, the lawyer may also provide estimates of (1) the likelihood of an outcome unfavorable to the client; and (2) the probable loss or range of loss if the client loses.

Chapter 18

INTERNAL ACCOUNTING CONTROLS

"The company accountant is shy and retiring. He's shy a quarter of a million dollars. That's why he's retiring."
— *Milton Berle*

Nobody — business or individual — likes to be victimized by theft or fraud, but it seems to happen often — trusted employees or agents embezzling millions of dollars, taking bribes or kickbacks to act improperly, conspiring to produce inaccurate financial records. One of accountants' most important tasks is to design accounting systems to minimize those kinds of losses. These systems are known as ***internal accounting controls***, or just ***internal controls***. Human nature being what it is, no accounting system can stop all fraud or theft, but good internal accounting controls can minimize losses.

Internal accounting controls are more than just good business practice; for many companies, they are a legal requirement. Congress has mandated internal controls for public companies since 1970, when it passed the Foreign Corrupt Practices Act. The Act requires public companies to keep accounting books and records that accurately reflect the transactions in which the company engages, and mandates a system of internal accounting controls.[1]

The Sarbanes-Oxley Act of 2002 added additional requirements designed to get the management and auditors of public companies more actively involved with internal accounting controls. Annual reports filed with the SEC by most large public companies must now include an assessment by the company's management of the effectiveness of the internal control system.[2] In addition, the Sarbanes-Oxley Act requires these companies' auditors to report on the company's internal controls.[3] A typical internal controls report looks something like this:

Report of Independent Registered Public Accounting Firm

We have audited X Corporation's internal control over financial reporting as of December 31, 2013, based on criteria established in *Internal Control — Integrated Framework* issued by the Committee of Sponsoring Organizations of the Treadway Commission (COSO). X Corporation's management is responsible for maintaining effective internal control over financial reporting and for its assessment of the effectiveness of internal control over financial

---

[1] *See* Securities Exchange Act of 1934 § 13(b)(2), 15 U.S.C. § 78m(b)(2).

[2] Sarbanes Oxley Act of 2002 § 404(a).

[3] Sarbanes Oxley Act of 2002 § 404(b).

reporting. Our responsibility is to express an opinion on the company's internal control over financial reporting based on our audit.

We conducted our audit in accordance with the standards of the Public Company Accounting Oversight Board (United States). Those standards require that we plan and perform the audit to obtain reasonable assurance about whether effective internal control over financial reporting was maintained in all material respects. Our audit included obtaining an understanding of internal control over financial reporting, assessing the risk that a material weakness exists, testing and evaluating the design and operating effectiveness of internal control based on the assessed risk, and performing such other procedures as we considered necessary in the circumstances. We believe that our audit provides a reasonable basis for our opinion.

A company's internal control over financial reporting is a process designed to provide reasonable assurance regarding the reliability of financial reporting and the preparation of financial statements for external purposes in accordance with generally accepted accounting principles. A company's internal control over financial reporting includes those policies and procedures that (1) pertain to the maintenance of records that, in reasonable detail, accurately and fairly reflect the transactions and dispositions of the assets of the company; (2) provide reasonable assurance that transactions are recorded as necessary to permit preparation of financial statements in accordance with generally accepted accounting principles, and that receipts and expenditures of the company are being made only in accordance with authorizations of management and directors of the company; and (3) provide reasonable assurance regarding prevention or timely detection of unauthorized acquisition, use, or disposition of the company's assets that could have a material effect on the financial statements.

Because of its inherent limitations, internal control over financial reporting may not prevent or detect misstatements. Also, projections of any evaluation of effectiveness to future periods are subject to the risk that controls may become inadequate because of changes in conditions, or that the degree of compliance with the policies or procedures may deteriorate.

In our opinion, X Corporation maintained, in all material respects, effective internal control over financial reporting as of December 31, 2013, based on the criteria established in *Internal Control — Integrated Framework* issued by the Committee of Sponsoring Organizations of the Treadway Commission (COSO).

We have also audited, in accordance with the standards of the Public Company Accounting Oversight Board (United States), the balance sheets of X Corporation as of December 31, 2013 and 2012, and the related statements of operations, comprehensive income, stockholders' equity, and cash flows for each of the three years in the period ended December 31, 2013 of X Corporation and our report dated January 30, 2014 expressed an unqualified opinion thereon.

/s/ Dense & Obtuse
Certified Public Accountants
January 30, 2014

In addition to these federal requirements, state corporate law decisions require corporate directors to take at least some responsibility for internal controls. In the well-known *Caremark* case, for example, the Delaware Chancery Court held that directors have a duty to ensure that the corporation has an internal control system reasonably designed to provide accurate information "concerning both the company's compliance with law and its business performance."[4]

THE ESSENCE OF INTERNAL CONTROLS

A detailed discussion of internal control systems is beyond the scope of this book. University accounting departments devote entire courses to this subject.[5] But the key to effective internal controls is to avoid putting all of a company's accounting functions into one set of hands. A business should keep three accounting responsibilities separated: (1) the custody of assets, (2) the recording of transactions regarding those assets, and (3) the authorization to dispose of those assets. Separating these functions makes it more difficult for a single person to defraud the company.

A company that allows one person to gain control over multiple accounting functions is asking for trouble. Consider the case of Donald Peterson, a 57-year old high school dropout who spent his entire career as a bookkeeper embezzling millions of dollars from small businesses which employed him.[6] He routinely had access to checks and he reconciled the bank statement. Few of the owners of the businesses he defrauded ever reviewed the bank statements[7] and none of the owners ever reviewed the cancelled checks. Because he had both custody of the checks and the responsibility to record and reconcile the checks, he could write checks to himself without discovery.

Or consider what Edward Campos did to the Los Angeles Dodgers baseball team. Campos was the Dodgers' payroll chief. The Dodgers allowed him to authorize the payroll, record the payments, and have custody of the paychecks. This monumental control deficiency allowed Campos to embezzle several hundred thousand dollars. His

---

[4] In Re Caremark Int'l, Inc. Derivative Litigation, 698 A.2d 959, 970 (Del. Ch. 1996).

[5] Before you criticize accounting professors for this, remember some of the subjects law schools devote entire courses to.

[6] *How Low-Key Style Let a Con Man Steal Millions From Bosses*, WALL St. J., Dec. 4, 1995, at B1.

[7] When an employer wanted to look at the bank statement, Peterson supplied a forged copy.

embezzlement was easily discovered in 1986 when Campos became ill and someone else had to perform his duties. The replacement discovered that some employees earning $7 per hour were supposedly receiving paychecks of nearly $2,000 each week.[8]

Even the strictest separation of functions can't protect against collusion. If several key employees combine to cheat the company, the prevention and detection of fraud become more difficult. No system is foolproof, and there's always a tradeoff between the cost of losses and the cost of prevention. For example, a store concerned about shoplifting losses could position armed guards at each aisle and order them to shoot any suspected shoplifter. This would eliminate most of the shoplifting, but the costs of such a policy would be much greater than the benefits.

Key Concepts to Remember

1. Internal accounting controls are designed to keep track of transactions and prevent fraud and wrongdoing.

2. Accounting controls are good business practice, but they are also required to some extent by federal securities law, including the Sarbanes-Oxley Act, and by state corporate law. The managers of public companies and the auditors of those companies' financial statements must assess the effectiveness of the company's internal controls.

3. The key to effective internal accounting controls is to keep three accounting responsibilities in separate hands: (1) the custody of assets, (2) the recording of transactions regarding those assets, and (3) the authorization to dispose of those assets. This separation makes it more difficult for a single person to defraud the company.

---

[8] Paul Feldman, *7 Accused of Embezzling $332,583 From Dodgers*, L.A. Times, Sept. 16, 1986, § 2, at 1.

Chapter 19

GOVERNMENTAL ACCOUNTING

"Government expands to absorb revenue — and then some."
— *Tom Wicker*

This book focuses on the financial statements of private companies and individuals, but many government agencies also prepare financial statements. Government agencies are very different from for-profit businesses and individuals like you and me,[1] so, as you might expect, generally accepted accounting principles for those entities are also different. The standard setter is even different. In fact, there are two different standard setters for government agencies — one for the federal government and one for state and local governments.

The authoritative accounting standard setter for state and local governments is the ***Governmental Accounting Standards Board (GASB)***. The GASB is a private organization whose board members are selected by the same foundation that selects the FASB's board members. The GASB issues a number of different accounting pronouncements; the most authoritative of those are called ***Statements of Governmental Accounting Standards***.[2]

The authoritative accounting standard setter for federal government agencies is the ***Federal Accounting Standards Advisory Board (FASAB)***. The FASAB was created by the federal government, although it now has a supermajority of non-federal-government members. Its most authoritative source of guidance is ***The FASAB Handbook of Accounting Standards and Other Pronouncements***.[3]

Both the GASB standards and the FASAB standards are still called generally accepted accounting standards, although usually with a qualifier that indicates they are for government agencies. For example, the financial statements of a federal agency would indicate they were prepared in accordance with generally accepted accounting principles for federal entities.

---

[1] For example, you and I cannot spend $1 trillion more than we earn each year. It would be nice to try, though; one year is all I would need.

[2] All of the GASB pronouncements are available online at www.gasb.org.

[3] The FASAB Handbook and other FASAB materials are available online at www.fasab.gov.

Key Concepts to Remember

1. Government agencies also prepare financial statements; the accounting standards for government financial statements differ from those for businesses or individuals.

2. Generally accepted accounting principles for state and local government agencies are set by the Governmental Accounting Standards Board (GASB).

3. Generally accepted accounting principles for federal government agencies are set by the Federal Accounting Standards Advisory Board (FASAB).

THE UNCERTAINTY OF ACCOUNTING

Chapter 20

THE UNCERTAINTY OF ACCOUNTING

"None of us really understand what's going on with all these numbers."
— *David Stockman*

INTRODUCTION

Accounting produces numbers, and numbers provide a reassuring sense of certainty and security.[1] Many law students believe that numbers aren't as malleable as the words they encounter in their casebooks, which some professors seem to be able to reshape to mean whatever they want. Six dollars is $6, they believe, and no amount of deconstruction is going to make it otherwise. But the numbers in financial statements aren't really that certain. Accounting, like the law, is subject to judgment, interpretation, and manipulation.

Mathematics is certain.[2] Problems of addition and subtraction require no judgment. Two plus two in base 10 is always four, absolutely, without exception. Natural science is certain.[3] When you drop a rock, it falls to the ground. Not even the U.S. Congress can repeal the law of gravity.

Accounting rules, on the other hand, are man-made; they vary from time to time and place to place. They can be changed if enough people don't like the results they produce. They require judgment and are subject to exceptions. Math works the same for accountants as it does for the rest of us; they just use it more creatively. Like the words in your casebooks, the numbers in accounting statements require interpretation. You can't accept them at face value; you have to poke around a little to see what they mean.

In this chapter, you will see some examples of the uncertainty of accounting and how accounting numbers can be legitimately manipulated. You won't become an expert on accounting manipulations; in fact, this chapter only covers some of the simplest possibilities. But you should learn enough to give up any remaining notions about the certainty and reliability of accounting, and I hope you will begin treating financial statements with the same skepticism you give legal opinions.[4]

---

[1] I get such a warm feeling when 6,795 gives me my warm milk and tucks me into bed every night.

[2] Mathematicians might disagree, but who pays any attention to mathematicians?

[3] If you're a natural scientist, you might disagree. Go complain to a mathematician.

[4] No, I don't mean not reading them. I'm talking about the skeptical way you treat legal opinions when you actually read them.

DEPRECIATION, DEPLETION, AND AMORTIZATION

In Chapter 9, we looked at depreciation, depletion, and amortization. When a company purchases an asset it expects to last for several years, the cost of that asset must be allocated as an expense over its useful life. That allocation is called depreciation, depletion, or amortization, depending on what kind of asset is involved.[5]

Depreciation introduces several uncertainties into accounting. First, you must estimate the asset's useful life — the period over which its cost will be spread. When you buy a computer for $2,000, what is its expected useful life to the company? Four years? Five years? Six years? Your estimate must be reasonably based on economic circumstances; you can't just choose a figure with no basis in reality, such as 400 years. But estimating useful life requires judgment, and reasonable people can differ.

Second, you must estimate the asset's salvage value. When you're finished with the computer, how much could you sell it for? $200? $400? $600? Again, this is a judgment call, and the value chosen will affect the amount of depreciation expense.

Assume that you're using the straight-line method of depreciation, allocating the depreciable cost of the computer equally over its useful life.[6] If you think the computer's useful life is four years, with a salvage value of $200, the annual depreciation expense will be $450 (($2,000 − $200) ÷ 4). If you estimate a useful life of six years and salvage value of $500, the annual depreciation expense will be only $250. It's the same computer, but the expense (and therefore net income) is different because your estimate is different.

Estimating an asset's useful life and salvage value make depreciation uncertain, but the greatest opportunity for manipulation comes in the choice of depreciation method. As you saw in Chapter 9, you can depreciate assets in several different ways — the straight-line method, the units-of-output method, the double-declining-balance method, and the sum-of-the-years'-digits method. Even if you are absolutely certain about the asset's useful life and salvage value, the depreciation expense each period will still depend on the method you choose.

INVENTORY

In Chapter 10, we considered inventory and the Cost of Goods Sold. When goods are sold, the cost of those goods is an expense. But if your inventory consists of a number of units purchased at different times for different prices, the cost of goods sold can vary depending on the accounting method you choose — the FIFO (first-in, first-out) method, the LIFO (last-in, first-out) method, or the average cost method. Each method can produce a different Cost of Goods Sold expense, net income, and balance sheet value for the remaining inventory.

---

[5] To simplify the discussion, I'll use the term "depreciation" to include all three.

[6] Recall that the annual depreciation expense is the computer's cost minus its salvage value, divided by the number of years of useful life.

CONTINGENCIES

Chapter 11 dealt with how to account for contingencies: events that may or may not happen at some time in the future. You learned that contingent losses sometimes must be recognized before they occur. If a contingent loss, such as losing a lawsuit, is probable to occur in the future, and the amount of the loss can be reasonably estimated, that estimated amount must be treated as a current expense.

The uncertainty this test introduces is obvious. First, the company, its accountants, and its attorneys must decide whether the contingency is probable: Are we likely to lose the lawsuit? This prediction of the future requires judgment, and reasonable people can differ.[7] Second, if the loss is probable, what's a reasonable estimate of the amount of the loss? Will we have to pay $45,000 damages if we lose the lawsuit, or $50,000, or $55,000? Again, reasonable people can differ.

One company might not recognize a contingent loss at all, concluding that it's not probable. Another company might decide that the identical contingency is probable, and recognize a loss of $50,000, its reasonable estimate of the amount. A third company might agree that the loss is probable, but conclude that a reasonable estimate of the amount is $40,000. The contingency is the same for all three companies, but their financial statements will be different.

HISTORICAL COST VERSUS MARKET VALUE

Finally, remember that accounting statement values are usually based on historical cost — what you paid for assets. An asset's value on the financial statements may not be its market value. For example, immediately after World War II, you could have purchased land in downtown Tokyo very cheaply. Let's assume you bought ten lots for $100,000. Today, those ten lots would be worth millions of dollars, but your balance sheet would still show their original purchase price, $100,000. If you sold the land and actually realized the profit, the gain would show up on your financial statements. As a result of the sale, the book value of the company's assets would change appreciably even though the economic value of those assets remains the same.

When you're looking at financial statements, particularly the balance sheet, you should keep this in mind. Many of the numbers you're looking at are history and may not tell you much about the current market values — the true economic worth — of the company's assets and liabilities.

AN EXAMPLE OF ACCOUNTING UNCERTAINTY

The best way to appreciate the uncertainty of accounting is to see it in action. Let's take two identical companies, run them through equivalent transactions, and see how we can use the rules of accounting to make them appear different. And we'll keep the transactions relatively simple to prove that accounting numbers can be manipulated even in uncomplicated transactions.

---

[7] Even accountants and attorneys, who are not reasonable people, can differ.

We'll call our two companies Alpha Company and Beta Company. They have identical assets and no liabilities. Their balance sheets at the end of 2014 are identical, as follows:

Alpha and Beta Companies
Balance Sheet
As of December 31, 2014

Assets		Liabilities and Shareholders' Equity	
Cash	$1,500,000	Liabilities	$0
Inventory	700,000	Equity	2,300,000
Land	100,000		
Total Assets	$2,300,000	Total Liabilities and Equity	$2,300,000

This is our starting point, and it's obviously a very simple one. Now let's look at what happens to these companies in 2015 and see how different we can make them look.

Transaction 1 — Purchase of a Computer System. In 2015, Alpha and Beta purchased identical computer systems for $50,000 cash.

Alpha estimated that the system has a useful life of ten years and a salvage value of $5,000. The depreciable cost is $50,000 − $5,000 = $45,000. Using the straight-line method of depreciation, Alpha's depreciation expense for the year is $4,500, 1/10 of the system's depreciable cost. The net book value of the system on Alpha's balance sheet, after subtracting the accumulated depreciation, is $45,500.

Beta estimated that the system has a useful life of eight years and a salvage value of $2,000. Beta uses the double-declining-balance method of calculating depreciation. Its depreciation expense for the year is $12,500 and the net book value of the system on Beta's balance sheet, after subtracting accumulated depreciation, is $37,500.

Transaction 2 — Changes to Inventory. At the beginning of 2015, each company owned 2,000 widgets, purchased a couple of years ago for $350 each (resulting in the Inventory value of $700,000 on the December 31, 2014 balance sheets). In 2015, each company purchased 1,000 more widgets for $500 a widget, and sold 1,000 widgets for $700 a widget.

The sales revenue for both companies is $700,000 ($700 × 1,000 widgets). Alpha determines its Cost of Goods Sold using the FIFO method of inventory valuation. Its Cost of Goods Sold (an expense) is $350,000 ($350 × 1,000 widgets). Its ending inventory (the book value of the Inventory on the balance sheet) will be $850,000 — the beginning inventory, $700,000, plus the purchases, $500,000, minus the Cost of Goods Sold, $350,000.

Beta determines its Cost of Goods Sold using the LIFO method of inventory valuation. Its Cost of Goods Sold is $500,000 ($500 × 1,000 widgets). Its ending inventory (the book value of the Inventory) will be $700,000 — the beginning inventory, $700,000, plus the purchases, $500,000, minus the Cost of Goods Sold, $500,000.

Transaction 3: Collectibility of Accounts Receivable. Each company sold its widgets on credit, rather than for cash, creating Accounts Receivable of $700,000. The buyers were identical for both companies.

Alpha estimates that 2% of these accounts receivable will not be collected. Its Uncollectible Accounts Expense is 2% of the total, $14,000. On the balance sheet, the book value of its Accounts Receivable will be offset by a $14,000 Allowance for Uncollectible Accounts.

Beta estimates that 5% of these accounts receivable will not be collected. Its Uncollectible Accounts Expense is 5% of the total, $35,000, and the book value of its Accounts Receivable will be offset by a $35,000 Allowance for Uncollectible Accounts.

Transaction 4: Land. At the beginning of 2015, each company owned undeveloped real estate in Los Angeles, purchased in 1914 for $100,000. This land is listed on the December 31, 2014 balance sheets at its historical cost.

In January, Alpha sold its land for $10 million cash. This sale increased Alpha's cash by $10 million, eliminated the $100,000 in the Land account, and produced a profit of $9,900,000 (the $10 million sales price minus the cost of the land). In December, Alpha decided to purchase a similar piece of property for $10 million. The subsequent purchase created a new Land account with a book value of $10 million and reduced Alpha's cash by $10 million. The net result of the two transactions is no change to the Cash account, a $9,900,000 profit, and an increase in the Land account from $100,000 to $10 million.

Beta kept its land throughout 2015, so its financial statements didn't change. Note that, although Alpha's and Beta's actions differ, the two companies are still in an identical position at the end of the year. Each owns a similar parcel of land and each has the same amount of cash.

The Result of these Transactions. Alpha and Beta began and finished the year in identical positions, but look at what happened to their financial statements. First, let's examine their respective income statements for 2015, set forth below:

Alpha Company
Income Statement
For Calendar Year 2015[8]

Revenues:		
Sales of Widgets	$700,000	
Sale of Land	10,000,000	
Total Revenues		$10,700,000
Expenses:		
Depreciation	$4,500	
Cost of Goods Sold	350,000	
Uncollectible Accounts	14,000	
Cost of Land Sold	100,000	
Total Expenses		468,500
Net Income		$10,231,500

Beta Company
Income Statement
For Calendar Year 2015

Revenues:		
Sales of Widgets	$700,000	
Total Revenues		$700,000
Expenses:		
Depreciation	$12,500	
Cost of Goods Sold	500,000	
Uncollectible Accounts	35,000	
Total Expenses		547,500
Net Income		$152,500

Note the differences. Alpha's income statement shows $10 million revenue from the sale of land and a corresponding expense of $100,000. Beta had no such sale, so nothing comparable appears on Beta's income statement. The depreciation expenses differ because of different estimates of useful life and salvage value and because the companies use different methods of depreciation. The costs of goods sold differ because the companies use different methods of valuing inventory, and the uncollectible accounts expenses differ because of different estimates of collectibility. The net result is that Alpha has a net income of $10,231,500 and Beta has a net income of only $152,500.[9] The companies' real financial positions are still identical at the end of the year, but the accounting statements look very different.

Now, compare the two companies' balance sheets as of the end of 2015. Again, the differences are dramatic:

---

[8] The land sale would be treated a little differently on Alpha's Income Statement than I have shown here. I have simplified things to make it easier to see the difference.

[9] The land sale obviously accounts for a large portion of this difference. But, even without the land sale, Alpha's net income would be more than twice Beta's net income.

Alpha Company
Balance Sheet
As of December 31, 2015

Assets			*Liabilities and Equity*	
Cash		$950,000	Liabilities	$0
Widgets		850,000	Equity	12,531,500
Land		10,000,000		
Computer	$50,000			
Less: Accum. Depr.	4,500	45,500		
Accts. Receiv.	700,000			
Less: Allowance for Uncollectible Accounts	14,000	686,000		
Total Assets		$12,531,500	Total Liabilities and Equity	$12,531,500

Beta Company
Balance Sheet
As of December 31, 2015

Assets			*Liabilities and Equity*	
Cash		$950,000	Liabilities	$0
Widgets		700,000	Equity	2,452,500
Land		100,000		
Computer	$50,000			
Less: Accum. Depr.	12,500	37,500		
Accts. Receiv.	700,000			
Less: Allowance for Uncollectible Accounts	35,000	665,000		
Total Assets		$2,452,500	Total Liabilities and Equity	$2,452,500

The net book value of Alpha's assets at the end of 2015 is $12,531,500, compared to $2,452,500 for Beta. The reasons for this difference? Their different inventory valuation methods produce different values for the widgets, even though they both have identical sets of widgets. Alpha's sale and purchase of land produces a different book value for the land, even though the two properties are substantially the same. The different approaches to depreciation affect the book value of the computer systems, and the different estimates of collectibility affect the book value of the accounts receivable. The two companies are identical in all respects, but their accounting statements are dramatically different.

These differences result from a few very simple transactions. No sophisticated financial sleight-of-hand was involved. If such simple transactions can produce such dramatic differences, imagine what huge, multimillion-dollar conglomerates can do with more sophisticated transactions and accounting techniques.

Always remember: accounting is neither certain nor free of manipulation, even if accountants strictly follow generally accepted accounting principles (GAAP). And never forget that it's also possible to manipulate financial figures the old-fashioned way — by lying. You always need to look behind the numbers.

Key Concepts to Remember

1. Even though it uses numbers, accounting is not certain in the same sense as mathematics and science. Accounting requires the exercise of judgment and is subject to manipulation.

2. The financial statements of two very similar companies can differ because they use different depreciation or inventory methods, because they estimate things such as salvage value, useful life, or the probability of a contingency differently, or because one recognizes an increase in asset value through a sale and the other one does not. More complicated financial manipulations introduce even more uncertainty.

3. Because of this uncertainty (and because of the possibility of fraud), one must always treat financial statements with suspicion. Look behind the numbers.

Section Six

OTHER VALUATION CONCEPTS

Chapter 21

COST ACCOUNTING

"Money will not buy you true love. On the other hand, money will buy you a lot of high-quality fake love."
— *Dave Barry*

COST ACCOUNTING

How much does it cost? This question, which parents have been asking for generations,[1] also concerns accountants. *Cost accounting* deals with the collection and interpretation of information about costs. The purpose of cost accounting is to determine the cost of particular products or operations. How much does it cost to produce a can of beans?[2] Which costs more — boxing cans of beans by hand or using an automatic boxing machine?

Cost accounting is extremely important to the managers of businesses. They want to minimize costs and maximize profits and they can't do that without reliable cost data. The idea of cost is also important to economists. Many economic analyses, including economic analyses of law, turn on notions of cost.

The determination and allocation of costs is a difficult accounting problem requiring a sophisticated knowledge of accounting. We won't review the details of cost accounting, only some of the basic principles lawyers and law students should know.

FIXED COSTS, VARIABLE COSTS, AND TOTAL COST

All costs — such as the costs of manufacturing a product, the costs of driving a car, or the costs of attending law school — can be split into two categories: *fixed costs* and *variable costs*. A *fixed cost* is one that remains unchanged despite changes in volume. "Volume" in this definition means the amount of the activity in question — such as the number of units of a product manufactured, the number of miles a car is driven, or the number of credit-hours of law school courses you take. Assume, for example, that you must buy a law dictionary to attend law school. The cost of the dictionary is a fixed cost of attending law school. Whether you take 3, 6, 9, 12, or any other number of credit-hours, you need only one dictionary. The cost of the dictionary is fixed. It does

---

[1] As in the following dialogue:

Child: "I gotta have the new Slappo 1500Z Atomic, Laser-Guided, Modulated Destructo Alien-Blaster."

Parent: "How much does it cost?"

Child: "Only $97,000."

[2] Insert your own bean-counter joke here.

not vary with the number of credit-hours you take.

A *variable cost* is one that increases and decreases as volume increases and decreases. The cost of the electricity you use to charge your computer so you can take notes in class is a variable cost of attending law school. It varies with the number of credit-hours you take. The more credit-hours you take, the more time you'll be using your computer to take notes,[3] and the more electricity you'll need.

The distinction between fixed and variable costs is a little fuzzy. Most costs categorized as fixed costs are not really fixed for all possible volumes. Consider, for example, the cost of building a factory to manufacture bicycles. The cost of building the factory is a fixed cost of manufacturing bicycles. It is the same whether the factory produces 1, 2, 3, or 1,000 bicycles.[4] At some point, however, the factory will be producing at full capacity. If the company wants to make more bicycles than that, it must build a new factory or expand the old one. The cost of the factory, like most fixed costs, is not really fixed for all possible amounts of production. Because of this problem, a fixed cost is better defined as a cost that does not change within a specified range of volume.

The *total cost* of any activity is the sum of all the fixed and variable costs. Thus, the total cost of attending law school for three years is the sum of all the costs you pay, whether fixed or variable, that are attributable to your law school attendance: the cost of tuition, books, antacid, and so on.

It may sound simple, but it's often hard to decide the exact cost of a particular activity. For example, when you go out to lunch with a classmate to discuss your Evidence class, is the cost of the lunch a cost of attending law school? You would have to eat even if you weren't attending law school, so the cost of eating isn't really a cost of law school. But what if you usually eat a brown-bag lunch and you went out to eat only because your classmate refused to discuss Evidence anywhere else? If that's the case, the only reason you incurred that additional cost is to learn Evidence.

Or consider a company that produces several different products. If the company wants to determine the total cost of producing each product, how much of the corporate officers' salaries should it allocate to each? If all the products are produced at the same factory, how much of the cost of electricity and other utilities should be allocated to each product? And what about the cost of the factory itself?

MEASURING COST PER UNIT: AVERAGE TOTAL COST AND MARGINAL COST

Total cost measures the total cost of any given volume — the total cost of driving your car 10,000 miles; the total cost of manufacturing 100,000 bicycles; the total cost of attending law school for three years. Two other cost concepts measure the cost *per*

---

[3] Yes, I know, but pretend you *do* take notes.

[4] Just the cost of the factory itself, not the costs to operate the factory. The operating costs — things like electricity and maintenance — do vary with the amount of activity.

unit — the cost of driving your car one mile, the cost to produce a single bicycle, the cost of one credit-hour of law school.

One measure of cost per unit, ***average total cost***, is simply the total cost of producing all units divided by the total number of units produced. If the total cost of driving your car 10,000 miles is $1,000, the average total cost is 10¢ per mile ($1,000 divided by 10,000 miles). If the total cost to produce 10 bicycles is $1,500, the average total cost is $150 per bicycle ($1,500 divided by 10 bicycles). If the total cost of 90 credit-hours of law school is $90 billion, the average total cost is $1 billion per credit-hour.[5]

Total cost, you will recall, is the sum of all fixed costs and all variable costs. Occasionally, average total cost is split into these two component elements. ***Average fixed cost*** is the sum of all fixed costs divided by the number of units. ***Average variable cost*** is the sum of all variable costs divided by the number of units. Since fixed costs plus variable costs equal total cost, the sum of the average fixed cost and the average variable cost must equal the average total cost.

Another measure of the cost of a unit is ***marginal cost.*** Average total cost measures the average cost of producing all of the units; marginal cost measures the cost of producing one particular unit. Marginal cost is the additional cost of producing a particular unit after the units that came before it have been produced.[6]

The marginal cost of driving the 10,000th mile in your car is the additional cost of going one more mile after you've already driven 9,999 — the cost of the small additional amount of gas and the slight additional wear on the car. The marginal cost of taking Business Associations in law school consists of the extra costs you incur just for Business Associations — the additional tuition, the cost of the casebook, the extraordinary boredom.[7] The marginal cost of producing the tenth bicycle is the additional cost incurred to produce the tenth bicycle after the company has already produced the first nine. If it costs $1,400 to produce nine bicycles and $1,500 to produce 10, the marginal cost of producing the tenth one is the additional $100. Note that this differs from the average total cost of producing the 10 bicycles, which is $150 per bicycle ($1,500 ÷ 10). This is primarily because the marginal cost does not include all the fixed costs that have already been incurred before the tenth unit is produced.

AN EXAMPLE: THE COST OF OPERATING A LAW SCHOOL

To help you understand these concepts, let's consider the cost of operating a new law school. Before a law school admits its first student, it must have a building with classrooms and office space, it must hire faculty to teach the courses, and it must hire

---

[5] Yes, I'm exaggerating. I teach at a state university, where the total cost of 90 credit-hours of law school for a resident of the state is only $39 billion.

[6] In spite of the name, marginal cost is *not* the cost book manufacturers incur to create the blank spaces on the edge of each page.

[7] I teach Business Associations and I assume that my students' boredom stems from the subject, not the teacher. My student research assistant (who is about to be fired) has a different theory.

administrators to run the school.[8] Assume that the school hires 10 faculty members and two administrators and builds a new building. All of this costs $2 million. Once a school admits students, it must also keep records for each student, which we'll assume costs $5 per student. You need other things, like a good psychiatrist, to run a law school, but, to keep it simple, assume that these are the only costs.

Assume that the school only admits one student. The total cost to educate that one law student is $2,000,005 — the cost of the building, faculty, and administrators, plus the record-keeping cost for that student. This is also the marginal cost of educating the first law student — the additional cost incurred to educate one law student instead of none. And this is also the average cost — the total cost of $2,000,005 divided by one student. Total cost, average cost, and marginal cost are identical when only one unit of output is produced.

If the school admits a second student, it doesn't have to build another building or hire additional faculty and administrators. The existing building, faculty, and administrators can easily accommodate both students. These costs are fixed costs; they don't vary with the number of students. The only additional cost associated with the second student is a slight increase in record-keeping; the school must now prepare and maintain records on the second student, at an additional cost of $5. The record-keeping cost is a variable cost; it varies with the number of students.

The total cost of educating two law students is $2,000,010. The average total cost of educating these two law students is $1,000,005 (the total cost, $2,000,010, divided by the number of students, two). However, the marginal cost of educating the second law student is only $5. The only additional cost to educate the second student is the record-keeping.

If the school adds a third student, it still doesn't need a new building or more faculty or administrators. The only additional cost is the additional record-keeping cost, $5. Thus, the marginal cost of educating the third student is only $5. The total cost of educating all three law students is $2,000,015. The average total cost of educating these three law students is approximately $666,672 (the total cost $2,000,015, divided by the number of students, three).

The same trend continues as the size of the class increases to 4, 5, 6, and more students. The costs of the building, the faculty, and the administrators do not increase; over this range, those costs are fixed. The only additional cost, a variable cost, is the cost of the extra paperwork for each student. The marginal cost of each additional student remains $5, so the total cost increases by $5 for each additional student, and the average total cost declines as we divide the large fixed costs by more and more students.

At some point, however, the number of students will get so large that more faculty and administrators, and perhaps also more classroom space,[9] will be needed. These

---

[8] I believe that faculty members are the most important component of a law school. My research assistant (who is being fired even as this footnote is written) believes that the most important component of a law school must be the administrators, who have to manage people like me.

[9] The need for more classroom space depends on the counterfactual assumption that students go to class.

costs, which are fixed over some range of students, increase after enrollment reaches a certain number. As I stated earlier, "fixed" costs are usually fixed only over a certain range of output. Once you exceed that output, the "fixed" costs increase.

Key Concepts to Remember

1. A fixed cost is one that doesn't change as volume changes.

2. A variable cost is one that does change as volume changes.

3. The total cost of any activity is the sum of all the fixed and variable costs.

4. The average total cost is the total cost divided by the number of units produced. The average fixed cost is the sum of all the fixed costs divided by the number of units produced. The average variable cost is the sum of all the variable costs divided by the number of units produced.

5. Marginal cost is the additional cost of producing one more unit beyond what you are already producing.

Chapter 22

PRESENT VALUE AND THE TIME VALUE OF MONEY

"A billion here, a billion there — pretty soon it adds up to real money."
— *Senator Everett Dirksen*

The next two chapters deal with principles of valuation used more by financial analysts than by accountants. Although they aren't technically accounting principles, they are still very important for lawyers and law students to know. In this chapter, we will explore present value, future value, and the time value of money. In the next chapter, you will learn about another important valuation concept, expected value.

THE TIME VALUE OF MONEY

A dollar received now is worth more than a dollar to be received sometime in the future. A dollar paid now costs more than a dollar to be paid sometime in the future. This critical idea is known as the *time value of money.*

Assume that I offer to give you $100 and I say you can have either U.S. dollars or Canadian dollars.[1] Since you're reasonably intelligent,[2] you know that U.S. and Canadian dollars aren't equivalent just because they're both called "dollars." You would check on the Internet for currency values and pick the one that is worth the most.

I now give you a second choice: you can take the $100 now or you can wait and receive it in one year. You should take the $100 now.

Why? One answer is that you may not trust me. I am, after all, a law professor. You may fear that, a year from now, I will change my mind and not pay you or, more likely, I will be broke and unable to pay you. If you take the money now, you don't have to deal with that risk. In the next chapter, we'll talk about the effect uncertainty and risk have on value. But, even if you were absolutely sure you'd get the money in a year, $100 now is still more valuable.

Like the Canadian dollars and the U.S. dollars, $100 now and $100 in one year are not equivalent. A dollar today is not the same as a dollar in the future. If you take the money now, you can spend it immediately; if you don't need it now, you can invest it and have more than $100 in a year.

---

[1] Ignore the obvious flaws in this hypothetical: No law professor has $100 cash to give away and, even if I did, the likelihood that I would give it to a student is infinitesimally small.

[2] You must be: you bought this book. (What do you mean you just borrowed it, you cheapskate? I have vacation plans; I was going to use all the royalties from this book to drive downtown.)

Assume you can earn 6% interest on any money you invest. The $100 I give you today would grow to $106 after a year, the original $100 plus the interest.[3] The *future value* in one year of $100 today is $106. To put it another way, if the annual interest rate is 6%, having $100 now is equivalent to having $106 in one year. Since $100 now is equivalent to *$106* in one year, you clearly prefer $100 now to *$100* in one year.

If the choice is between $100 now and $100 *two* years from now, the difference is even greater. If you take $100 now and invest it at 6% interest, you would have $106 after one year. If you reinvest the $106 and earn the same 6% interest for the second year, you would have $112.36 by the end of the second year. This is clearly better than receiving $100 two years from now.

Notice that you earn $6 interest in the first year, and $6.36 interest in the second year. In the second year, you're earning 6% interest not only on the original $100, but also on the $6 interest you earned in the first year. The extra 36¢ is the interest on your first year's interest (6% of $6.00). This interest on interest is known as *compound interest*.[4]

The future value of any amount of money is simply the original amount plus the interest you could earn on it. The future value one year from now of $1 today is

$$FV_{(1 \text{ year})} \quad = \quad \$1 \times (1 + r),$$

where r is the annual rate of interest expressed in decimal form (for example, 4% equals .04). Thus, if the rate of interest is 10%, the future value of $1 in one year is

$$
\begin{aligned}
FV \quad &= \quad \$1 \times (1 + .10) \\
&= \quad \$1 \times 1.10 \\
&= \quad \$1.10
\end{aligned}
$$

More generally, the future value in one year of any amount A is

$$FV_{(1 \text{ year})} \quad = \quad A \times (1 + r).$$

Applying the formula, if the rate of interest is 5%, the value of $150 after one year of interest is

$$
\begin{aligned}
FV \quad &= \quad \$150 \times (1 + .05) \\
&= \quad \$150 \times 1.05 \\
&= \quad \$157.50
\end{aligned}
$$

The future value in two years of any amount A is simply the value after the first year multiplied by the interest factor again:

$$FV_{(2 \text{ years})} \quad = \quad A \times (1 + r) \times (1 + r).$$

---

[3] This assumes that you don't have to pay taxes on your interest income. If you have to pay taxes, your interest income after taxes would be approximately three cents.

[4] If interest is paid only on the principal amount invested and not on the interest, it's known as *simple interest*.

The future value in three years of that same amount would just be the value after the second year multiplied by the interest factor again:

$$FV_{(3 \text{ years})} = A \times (1 + r) \times (1 + r) \times (1 + r)$$

To determine how much any given amount will be worth n years from now, you simply multiply by the interest factor, $(1 + r)$, n times. Using exponential notation, the formula to determine the future value of A dollars at the end of n years is:

$$FV_{(n \text{ years})} = A \times (1 + r)^n.$$

For those of you unfamiliar with exponential notation, the superscript n in the formula is simply another way of indicating that you should multiply by $(1 + r)$ n times. Thus, the future value of $50 after five years, if the rate of interest is 6%, is:

$$
\begin{aligned}
FV &= \$50 \times (1 + .06)^5 \\
&= \$50 \times (1.06) \times (1.06) \times (1.06) \times (1.06) \times (1.06) \\
&= \$66.91
\end{aligned}
$$

I don't recommend that you solve equations like this using pencil and paper. You can do this easily on a computer or calculator. Many calculators and computer programs have future value functions that will do all the work for you. You don't even have to know the formula. You just input the amount, the number of years, and the interest rate. But, even if your computer is doing the work for you, it's important that you understand what's going on, so you know what the future value number means.

PRESENT VALUE

Present value is just the reverse of future value. Future value measures the value in the future of a payment now; present value measures the value now of a payment to be made in the future. Present value asks how much you would need to invest right now to have a specified amount in the future. To calculate present value, you just reverse the future value calculations. If $100 today is worth $106 in one year, then the present value of $106 to be paid in one year is $100.

The interest rate used to calculate present value is called the *discount rate.* The discount rate is essentially the return the person could have earned on the money in the time prior to payment. It measures how much the delay in receiving money costs a person.

To determine the present value of an amount to be paid or received in the future, you divide by the interest factor instead of multiplying by it. The present value of $1 to be received in one year is

$$PV = \frac{\$1}{(1 + r),}$$

where r is the rate of interest (the discount rate). Thus, if the discount rate is 7%, the present value of $1 to be received in one year is

$$PV = \frac{\$1}{(1 + .07)}$$

$$= \frac{\$1}{1.07}$$

$$= \$0.93 \text{ (approximately)}$$

One dollar in one year is equivalent to 93¢ now. If you had 93¢ now and invested it at 7%, it would equal (approximately) $1 in one year. The present value of $1 to be received in *two* years is

$$PV = \frac{\$1}{(1 + r) \text{ x } (1 + r).}$$

The present value of $1 to be received in *three* years is

$$PV = \frac{\$1}{(1 + r) \text{ x } (1 + r) \text{ x } (1 + r).}$$

To generalize, the present value of any amount $A to be received in n years is

$$PV = \frac{A}{(1 + r)^n.}$$

For example, if the discount rate is 6%, the present value of $750 to be received in five years is

$$PV = \frac{\$750}{(1 + .06)^5}$$

$$= \frac{\$750}{(1.06)(1.06)(1.06)(1.06)(1.06)}$$

$$= \frac{\$750}{1.3382}$$

$$= \$560.44 \text{ (approximately)}$$

In other words, if your discount rate is 6%, a payment of $750 in five years is equivalent to $560.44 today.

THE PRESENT VALUE OF A SERIES OF PAYMENTS

You can also calculate the present value of a series of payments to be made at different times in the future. Assume, for example, that an investment will pay back $100 at the end of the first year, $250 at the end of the second year, $50 at the end of the third year, and $400 at the end of the fourth and final year. The present value of this investment is simply the sum of the present values of each payment.

If the discount rate is 5%, then the present value of the first $100 payment, using the formula, is $100/(1.05) = \$95.24$. The present value of the $250 payment at the end of year two is $250/(1.05)^2 = \$226.76$. The present value of the $50 payment at the end of year three is $50/(1.05)^3 = \$43.19$. The present value of the $400 payment at the end of year four is $400/(1.05)^4 = \$329.08$. The present value of the entire investment is simply the sum of all these individual present values:

$$PV = \frac{100}{(1.05)} + \frac{250}{(1.05)^2} + \frac{50}{(1.05)^3} + \frac{400}{(1.05)^4}$$
$$= \$95.24 + \$226.76 + \$43.19 + \$329.08$$
$$= \$694.27$$

If each of the annual payments in a series is exactly the same amount, the stream of payments is known as an **annuity**. For example, a promise to pay someone $100 a year at the end of each of the next six years is an annuity. It's easier to work with annuities than it is to work with uneven payments. You don't have to calculate the present value of each year's payment; there's a formula that calculates the present value of the entire annuity.[5] But the concept is essentially the same.

THE PERIOD OF COMPOUNDING

To determine future values and present values accurately, you need to know how often interest is **compounded** — that is, how often it is credited to the account. Because of compound interest (interest on interest), the compounding period affects the amount of interest paid. For example, if you put $100 each in two different bank accounts, one paying 12% interest compounded monthly and the other paying 12% interest compounded annually,[6] the amounts in the two accounts won't be the same at the end of the year.

In the account where interest is compounded annually, nothing will happen until the end of the year. At that point, the bank will calculate your interest (multiplying your $100 by the annual interest rate), and will add the interest to your account. The value of that account after one year will be:

$$FV = \$100 \times (1 + .12)$$
$$= \$112.00$$

In the account where interest is compounded monthly, the bank will add interest to your account at the end of each month. The monthly interest rate is simply one-twelfth of the annual rate (12% ÷ 12 = 1%). Thus, at the end of the first month, the amount in your account will be:

$$FV = \$100 \times (1 + .01)$$
$$= \$101.00$$

At the end of the second month, the bank will again add interest to your account, multiplying the amount in the account by the monthly interest rate. But notice that they're now paying you interest not just on your original $100, but also on the first

---

[5] You really don't want to know, but if you insist, the present value of an annuity is $(1 - (1/(1 + r)^n))/r$. (Sorry you asked now, aren't you?) Most financial calculators and computer programs can calculate the present value of annuities for you, so you don't have to use this complicated formula.

[6] No, I don't know where to find a bank that pays interest of 12%. If I did, I wouldn't waste my time writing this book.

month's $1.00 interest. At the end of the second month, the amount in your account will be:

$$FV = \$101 \times (1 + .01)$$
$$= \$102.01$$

Because of compound interest, you will have more at the end of the year in the account that is compounded monthly than in the account that is compounded only annually, even though the annual interest rate is the same for both accounts. The more often interest is compounded, the greater the total interest. In this example, the difference after one year is about 68¢.

Luckily, you can use the same formulas no matter what the period of compounding is. Remember the basic formulas for future value and present value:

$$FV = A \times (1 + r)^n$$
$$PV = \frac{A}{(1 + r)^n}$$

where A is the amount to be paid or received, n is the number of periods, and r is the interest or discount rate for each period.

When you first saw these formulas, n was the number of *years* and r was the *annual* interest rate. We were assuming that interest was compounded annually. If the period of compounding is something other than a year, you use the same formula, but n in the formula is the number of days or the number of months or whatever the compounding period is, and r is the interest rate for that period (per day or per month or whatever).

If the annual interest rate is 12%, but interest is compounded monthly, then the *monthly* rate of interest is 1%. The present value of $500 to be received in six months (six periods of compounding) is:

$$PV = \frac{\$500}{(1 + .01)^6}$$
$$= \$0.93 \text{ (approximately)}$$

If the annual interest rate is 8%, but interest is compounded quarterly, the *quarterly* rate of interest is 2%. The future value in one year (four quarters) of $10 today is:

$$FV = \$10 \times (1.02)^4$$
$$= \$10.82 \text{ (approximately)}$$

Often, the examples you'll see in law school will assume annual compounding, but you should always check before you start plugging numbers into the formulas.[7]

---

[7] Present values are almost always calculated using annual compounding.

AN APPLICATION: LOST WAGES

The concept of present value is often used to calculate damages, such as the value of lost wages. Assume that I am eating my breakfast and texting while driving to the law school.[8] I run over one of my colleagues, Professor Smith; due to his injuries, Professor Smith is unable to work for the rest of his life.[9]

At the time of his injury, Smith was 40 years old; he would have retired at age 65. If Smith was earning $25,000 a year when he was injured and would have continued to earn $25,000 a year for the rest of his life, how much would I have to pay to compensate Smith for his lost wages?[10] (Just for his lost wages, not for any other damages he might have suffered.)

Smith's total wages for the 25 years of work he had remaining would have been $625,000 ($25,000 a year times 25 years). But, due to the time value of money, awarding Smith a lump sum of $625,000 now would drastically overcompensate him. Each $25,000 payment Smith would have received in future years is worth less than $25,000 now.

Consider the $25,000 that Smith would have received a year from now. If Smith receives $25,000 now, he could invest it and have more than $25,000 in a year (when he would have received the wages). For example, if Smith could earn 5%, the $25,000 we give him now would become $26,250 ($25,000 × 1.05) in one year.[11] That's more than he would have made if he were still working. The $25,000 to Smith for the lost wages two years from now would become $27,562.50 ($25,000 × 1.05 × 1.05) by the time he would have received those wages. Paying Smith $25,000 now for each year of future wages overcompensates him.

To accurately measure the present cost to Smith of losing his future wages, we need to discount those wages to a present value. The damages for the wages he would have received next year are not $25,000, but the present value of that $25,000, approximately $23,809 ($25,000 ÷ 1.05). The damages for the second year's lost wages are the present value of $25,000 to be received in two years, $22,675.74 ($25,000 ÷ 1.05^2).

If we calculate the present value of each year's wages, we can determine the amount the defendant must pay Smith now to compensate Smith for all of his lost future wages. That amount, assuming a 5% discount rate, is $352,348.61, not $625,000. Notice how big a difference the time value of money can make when a long period of time is involved.

---

[8] Not really. I'm not that stupid. I usually read the newspaper while driving to work.

[9] Not that Smith worked much before I ran him over.

[10] To simplify the calculation, I assume a constant wage and no inflation. You could calculate the present value of Smith's lost wages without these assumptions, but you would have to factor in the expected value and timing of any raises, and discount for inflation.

[11] To keep things simple, this calculation assumes that Smith is paid his entire salary once at the end of the year. If Smith's wages are paid on a monthly or weekly basis, we'd have to use a month or a week as the period and a monthly or weekly discount rate.

THE LIMITS OF PRESENT VALUE AND THE USE OF SENSITIVITY ANALYSIS

Used carefully and cautiously, present value is a powerful tool. But present value is only as good as the numbers used to calculate it. If you put garbage into the formulas, you get garbage out. Relying on such calculations without careful analysis is just as dangerous as not understanding them at all. As with accounting statements, do not assume that a claim is accurate just because it's dressed up in numbers and mathematics is involved.

Present value calculations depend on the accuracy of (1) the payment amounts and (2) the discount rate. If the amounts to be paid or received are wrong, the present value will be wrong. In the lost wages example above, if Smith's salary for the next 25 years would have been $30,000 instead of $25,000, the present value we calculated using the $25,000 figure would be meaningless.

The discount rate can also have a tremendous effect on present value. The higher the discount rate, the lower the present value. The lower the discount rate, the higher the present value. If, in the lost wages example, the discount rate should have been 7% instead of 5%, the present value of Smith's wages would be only $291,339.58. That's $61,000 less than what we calculated using a 5% discount rate. The longer the period of time involved, the greater the effect of an improper discount rate.

Fortunately, there is a way to determine how sensitive present values are to the numbers you're using to calculate them. This method is known as ***sensitivity analysis.*** To do a sensitivity analysis, you simply input plausible alternative numbers and see how drastically those alternative numbers affect the result — in other words, how sensitive your result is to the numbers you're using.

The exact amount of a future payment may be uncertain, but you may be able to calculate a range within which you are sure the amount of the payment will fall. What happens if you use other figures in that range? Similarly, you may not be confident that the discount rate you chose is exactly correct, but you're sure the discount rate falls within a certain range. What happens if you use other rates in that range?

Consider Smith's lost wages again. Your best estimate of Smith's future salary is $25,000, but it could range from $20,000 to $30,000. Your best estimate of the appropriate discount rate is 5%, but it could be anything from 4% to 8%. Using your best estimates ($25,000 and 5%), we previously determined that the present value of Smith's lost wages is approximately $352,349. The following table presents a sensitivity analysis of this calculation.

SENSITIVITY ANALYSIS
PRESENT VALUE OF SMITH'S LOST WAGES

Discount Rate	Annual Salary		
	$20,000	$25,000	$30,000
4%	$312,442	$390,552	$468,662
5%	$281,879	**$352,349**	$422,818
6%	$255,667	$319,584	$383,501
7%	$233,072	$291,340	$349,608
8%	$213,496	$266,869	$320,243

The table shows the present value of Smith's lost wages with various plausible combinations of salary and discount rates. (The original result is in bold.) As you can see, depending on the numbers we choose, the possible present values vary significantly — from a low of $213,496 to a high of $468,662. Unless you're very sure of your numbers, you should be cautious in using the original estimate.

Key Concepts to Remember

1. Time value of money: A dollar today is worth more than a dollar to be paid or received sometime in the future.

2. Interest paid on both principal and past interest is known as compound interest.

3. The future value of any current amount is the amount that the current amount will grow to by the future date.

4. The formula for future value (FV) is $FV = A \times (1 + r)^n$, where A is the current amount, r is the interest rate per period, and n is the number of periods.

5. Present value is the value now of a payment to be made or received sometime in the future. In other words, how much would we need to invest right now to have the specified amount at the specified point in the future? The discount rate is the interest rate at which we could invest.

6. The formula for present value (PV) is $PV = A \div (1 + r)^n$, where A is the future amount at the end of n periods and r is the discount rate.

7. The accuracy of future value and present value calculations depends on the accuracy of the numbers we use. However, we can use sensitivity analysis to see how changes in the numbers affect the result.

Chapter 23

EXPECTED VALUE

"It is probable that many things will happen contrary to probability."
— *Unknown*

In the last chapter you learned about present value — how to value future payments in terms of present dollars. Another useful valuation concept is ***expected value.*** Expected value is used to value uncertain outcomes. It is, in essence, an average of the possible outcomes, weighted by the probability that each outcome will occur.

To understand expected value, assume that I offer to bet with you on the roll of a die. I will roll it once: if a one or two comes up, I'll pay you $15; if any other number comes up,[1] you have to pay me $9. Should you take this bet?

The outcome when I roll the die is uncertain, but, if the die is fair,[2] each of the six numbers is equally likely. There's a 1/6 chance that a one will come up, a 1/6 chance that a two will come up, and so on. You win if either a one or a two comes up, so there's a two out of six, or 1/3, chance that you will win $15. I win if any of the other four numbers comes up, so there's a four out of six, or 2/3, chance that you will have to pay me $9. If I rolled the die again and again, you'd receive $15 approximately 1/3 of the time and you'd pay me $9 approximately 2/3 of the time.

Expected value measures the average outcome of uncertain events such as rolling the die. You calculate expected value by multiplying each possible outcome times the probability that the outcome will occur. Since one of the outcomes must occur, all of the probabilities must add up to one (100%). In the die example, the two possible outcomes for you are a $15 win, with a probability of 1/3, and a $9 loss, with a probability of 2/3. The expected value to you of the bet is:

$$
\begin{aligned}
EV \quad &= \quad (\$15 \times 1/3) + (-\$9 \times 2/3) \\
&= \quad \$5 + -\$6 \\
&= \quad -\$1
\end{aligned}
$$

On average, you lose $1 on each roll of the die. If I rolled the die an extremely large number of times, you'd win $15 about 1/3 of the time and you'd pay $9 about 2/3 of the time, but you would have an average loss of $1 on each roll. This is not a good bet for you unless you're planning to cheat.

Notice that you never lose exactly $1 on any roll. The only two possibilities are winning $15 or losing $9. The -$1 expected value is only an average, and the average

---

[1] If any number higher than six comes up, you probably shouldn't bet with me anymore.

[2] This is probably not a safe assumption when you're betting with a law professor.

doesn't have to be one of the possibilities (which is why the average family can have 1.9 children even though there are few headless children running around[3]).

Understanding expected value is clearly helpful when you're betting with unsavory law professors, but how is it relevant to your legal studies? Here's one example: You represent the plaintiff in a tort case.[4] The defendant's lawyer offers $110,000 cash to settle the case; you're convinced this is her best offer. Should your client accept the offer or try the case?

You estimate that the probability of a verdict in favor of the defendant is about 25%. There's a 50% chance that the plaintiff will win and receive damages of $120,000 and a 25% chance that the plaintiff will win and receive damages of $320,000. Assume that it will cost $20,000 in costs and attorneys' fees to try the case and that, win or lose, each party must pay his own attorneys' fees and costs.

The net gain or loss to the plaintiff is the amount of damages received less the costs and attorneys' fees he has to pay. Thus, there's a 25% chance that the plaintiff will lose $20,000 ($0 − $20,000), a 50% chance that the plaintiff will win $100,000 ($120,000 − $20,000), and a 25% chance that the plaintiff will win $300,000 ($320,000 − $20,000). The expected value to the plaintiff of going to trial is:

$$
\begin{aligned}
EV \ &= \ (.25 \times \text{-}20{,}000) + (.50 \times 100{,}000) + (.25 \times 300{,}000) \\
&= \ \text{-}5{,}000 + 50{,}000 + 75{,}000 \\
&= \ \$120{,}000
\end{aligned}
$$

The expected value of going to trial, $120,000, is greater than the settlement offer, $110,000.

Of course, I have omitted two important elements of valuation that the client would want to consider in deciding whether to settle. First, the timing of the payments differs. The settlement will be paid now; the damages won't be paid until sometime in the future, after the conclusion of the trial. To compare the two, you'd want to discount the damages to their present value. Later in this chapter, we'll consider how to combine present value and expected value in a single calculation.

The second consideration is that the settlement amount is fixed and guaranteed. You know for sure what you're getting if you take the settlement. Going to trial is riskier: the plaintiff might gain as much as $300,000 or he might lose $20,000. The plaintiff might want to consider this risk in deciding whether to settle.

Expected value analysis is common in business and government. A government agency might calculate the expected value of adopting a new regulation when it is uncertain what the exact effect of the regulation will be. A business might calculate the expected value of introducing a new product when it is uncertain exactly how profitable the product will be. An investor might calculate the expected value of an investment when the return on the investment is uncertain.

---

[3] Brainless perhaps, but not headless.

[4] Not a torte case, which is much yummier.

For example, assume that an oil company is deciding whether to drill for oil on property it owns. Drilling will cost $100,000. The company's geologist is not sure if there's oil under the land or, if so, how much oil. However, after reviewing the geological data,[5] the geologist can provide some estimates.

The geologist thinks there's a 25% chance that the property contains no oil at all, in which case the company incurs the $100,000 cost of drilling and gets no income (a $100,000 loss). There's a 25% chance that the property contains enough oil to produce revenue of $40,000 (a $60,000 loss, after subtracting the cost of drilling). There's a 30% chance that the property contains enough oil to produce revenue of $120,000 (a net profit of $20,000). There's a 20% chance that the property contains enough oil to produce revenue of $300,000 (a net profit of $200,000).

To simplify matters, assume that drilling, removing the oil, and selling it all occur instantaneously, so we don't have to worry about calculating present values.[6] The expected value of drilling is:

$$EV = (.25 \times -\$100,000) + (.25 \times -\$60,000) + (.30 \times \$20,000) + (.20 \times \$200,000)$$
$$= \$6,000.$$

If the geologist's estimates are reliable, drilling should be profitable on average.

THE LIMITS OF EXPECTED VALUE AND THE USE OF SENSITIVITY ANALYSIS

Expected values, like present values, are only as reliable as the numbers used to calculate them. Expected value calculations depend on the accuracy of (1) the possible outcomes and their values and (2) the probabilities assigned to each outcome. If a possible outcome is overlooked or the gain or loss associated with an outcome is misestimated, the resulting expected value will be unreliable. If the probabilities assigned to each possible outcome are wrong, the resulting expected value will also be wrong.

As with present values, *sensitivity analysis* can be used to determine how sensitive expected values are to the numbers used to calculate them. A sensitivity analysis of an expected value calculation is done in much the same way as a sensitivity analysis of a present value calculation. You try plausible alternative numbers and see how drastically the alternative numbers affect the result.

To understand how sensitivity analysis works for expected values, reconsider the oil drilling example. The company's geologist estimates the probabilities of finding oil on the company's property and the associated profit to the company (after subtracting drilling costs) as follows:

[5] I use the term "geological data" to disguise the fact that I don't have the slightest idea what geologists look at.

[6] Or assume that the numbers given are already present values.

No Oil	25%	-$100,000
Some Oil	25%	-$60,000
More Oil	30%	$20,000
Bonanza[7]	20%	$200,000

We calculated earlier that, given these probabilities and outcomes, the expected value of drilling is $6,000.

These are the geologist's best estimates of probabilities and outcomes, but they could be wrong. The geologist has calculated three sets of probabilities: the best estimates, an optimistic scenario, and a pessimistic scenario, as follows:

	Optimistic	*Best Estimate*	*Pessimistic*
No Oil	20%	25%	30%
Some Oil	20%	25%	30%
More Oil	35%	30%	25%
Bonanza	25%	20%	15%

The geologist also believes that the profit to the company could vary. Drilling costs might be slightly more or less than the estimates and the price of oil might vary slightly. The geologist has also calculated optimistic and pessimistic scenarios of the net returns to the company, as follows:

	Optimistic	*Best Estimate*	*Pessimistic*
No Oil	-$80,000	-$100,000	-$120,000
Some Oil	-$40,000	-$60,000	-$80,000
More Oil	$40,000	$20,000	$0
Bonanza	$220,000	$200,000	$180,000

We can use the geologist's alternative figures to do a sensitivity analysis. If we combine each of the three sets of probabilities with each of the three sets of monetary outcomes, we can produce nine different expected values. The expected value of each combination appears in the following table:[8]

SENSITIVITY ANALYSIS
EXPECTED VALUE OF OIL DRILLING

Outcomes	Probabilities		
	Optimistic	Best Estimate	Pessimistic
Optimistic	$45,000	$26,000	$7,000
Best Estimate	$25,000	$6,000	-$13,000
Pessimistic	$5,000	-$14,000	-$33,000

As you can see, although most of the combinations result in gains, the possible

---

[7] Given the oil example, a more appropriate label might be "The Beverly Hillbillies." (If you understand this, you need to spend more time studying and less time watching very old TV shows.)

[8] If you want some practice calculating expected values, try to verify one or more of the numbers in the table.

expected values range from a net gain of $45,000 to a net loss of $33,000.

RISK

One problem with using expected values is that they don't take into account *risk* — the variability of the possible outcomes. Two identical expected values can mask very different sets of outcomes.

Pretend that you're a top executive of the Disgusting Toy Company. You have to choose between two proposed toy guns your engineers have designed: the Safety Shooter and the Destructo Destroyer.[9] Each toy costs the same amount to make and the expected value of the profits is the same for both, $10 million. You cannot choose one over the other on the basis of expected values because their expected values are the same.

To understand why risk matters, let's look at the probabilities and possible outcomes underlying those identical expected values. The Safety Shooter is a fairly traditional toy. It won't excite kids, but it's a safe, conservative bet. There's a 50% chance that it will produce profits of $11 million and a 50% chance that it will produce profits of $9 million. The expected value of its profits is:

$$\begin{aligned} \text{EV} &= (\$11 \text{ million} \times .5) + (\$9 \text{ million} \times .5) \\ &= \$5.5 \text{ million} + \$4.5 \text{ million} \\ &= \$10 \text{ million} \end{aligned}$$

The Destructo Destroyer is a much more exciting toy. The kids will love it. Unfortunately, it has a slight problem. The engineers think there's about a 10% chance that some of the Destructo Destroyers will blow up, causing great damage and resulting in great liability for the company. If the Destructo Destroyer works (a 90% probability), the profits will be tremendous, approximately $100 million. If it doesn't work and the company has to pay for the injuries (a 10% probability), the loss to the company will be approximately $800 million. The Destructo Destroyer's expected value is:

$$\begin{aligned} \text{EV} &= (\$100 \text{ million} \times .9) + (-\$800 \text{ million} \times .1) \\ &= \$90 \text{ million} + -\$80 \text{ million} \\ &= \$10 \text{ million} \end{aligned}$$

The expected values are the same, but the Destructo Destroyer is much riskier; the possible outcomes associated with it are much more variable.

In calculating expected value, $10 million is $10 million. The variability of the possible outcomes — the problem of risk — is not considered. But, in most situations, people don't like risk, everything else being equal. Most people would prefer the Safety Shooter, even though the expected values are the same, because they don't want to risk injuring small children.

---

[9] I realize that some parents object to toy guns, but I played with toy guns when I was young, and look how I turned out. . . . On second thought, maybe those who object to toy guns have a good point.

When you're working with expected values, you should also consider the risk associated with each choice. Risk, like expected value, can be measured, but measurements of risk go beyond the basics to be covered in this book.

COMBINING PRESENT VALUE AND EXPECTED VALUE

Present value and expected value calculations are not mutually exclusive. The two can be combined to value uncertain future outcomes.

Assume that you're trying to value a possible investment. You invest $100 today and you will receive some amount back in exactly one year, but the amount you'll get back is uncertain. You think there's a 50% chance that you'll only get your original $100 back. There's a 25% chance that you'll do better and receive $250 back, and a 25% chance that you'll get nothing at all, not even the $100 you originally invested.

To value this investment, you first need to translate the possible future receipts into present values. Assume that your discount rate is 10%. The present value of the $100 outcome is

$$PV \quad = \quad \frac{100}{(1 + .10)}$$
$$\quad = \quad \$90.91.$$

The present value of the $250 outcome is

$$PV \quad = \quad \frac{250}{(1 + .10)}$$
$$\quad = \quad \$227.27.$$

The present value of the $0 outcome is

$$PV \quad = \quad \frac{0}{(1 + .10)}$$
$$\quad = \quad \$0.[10]$$

Now that we have converted each possible outcome into a present value, we can calculate an expected value of those present values, or ***expected present value.*** We do this in the same way we calculate any other expected value, by multiplying each outcome by its probability and adding the products. The expected present value of the investment is

$$EPV \quad = \quad (.5 \times \$90.91) + (.25 \times \$227.27) + (.25 \times \$0)$$
$$\quad = \quad \$102.28$$

Since you invest only $100 and expect to get back an average of $102.28, this is a profitable investment.

---

[10] The present value of any zero outcome is always zero. Zero today is worth zero tomorrow.

Notice that we calculated present values first, then calculated an expected value of those present values. If all of the possible outcomes occur at the same time, you can do the calculation in the opposite order — first doing the expected value calculation, then converting that result into a present value. However, when the different outcomes occur at different times, this won't work, so you should always do the present value part of the calculations first.

Key Concepts to Remember

1. Expected value is used to value uncertain outcomes. It is, in essence, a weighted average of all the possible outcomes.

2. To calculate expected value, multiply each outcome by its probability, then total each of these products.

3. As with present values, sensitivity analysis can be used to determine how sensitive expected values are to the numbers used to calculate them.

4. Expected value calculations do not take risk into account. Two possibilities with the same expected value can vary greatly in risk.

5. Expected value can be combined with present value to calculate an expected present value. First, calculate the present value of each possible outcome, then determine the expected value of those present values.

GLOSSARY

Accelerated depreciation: Depreciation methods that allocate the cost of an asset as depreciation expense more rapidly than straight-line depreciation. *Compare* Straight-line depreciation. *See* Depreciation.

Account: A record of debits and credits relating to a particular asset, liability, or type of equity.

Accounting Principles Board (APB): A predecessor of the Financial Accounting Standards Board as accounting standard-setter, established by the American Institute of Certified Public Accountants.

Accounting Series Releases: The predecessors to the SEC's Financial Reporting Releases. *See* Financial Reporting Releases.

Accounting Standards Codification: The FASB's codification of generally accepted accounting principles. *See* Financial Accounting Standards Board.

Accrual basis of accounting: An accounting method that recognizes revenues when they are earned by sales or services and recognizes expenses when they provide benefits, not when cash is paid or received. This is the most common basis of accounting. *Compare* Cash basis of accounting. *See also* Accrual, Deferral; Matching principle; Revenue recognition principle.

Accrual: Recognizing revenues or expenses before the company receives (in the case of revenue) or pays (in the case of expenses) any cash or property. *Compare* Deferral.

Accumulated deficit: The name of the Retained Earnings account when it has a negative balance. *See* Retained earnings.

Accumulated depreciation: The cumulative depreciation expense for an asset or category of assets. *See* Depreciation, Book value.

Additional paid-in capital: One of the corporate equity accounts. The amount paid for corporate stock in excess of the par value of that stock. Also called "Paid-in capital in excess of par value" or, in some legal sources, "Capital surplus."

Adverse audit opinion: An audit opinion issued when the auditor finds that the financial statements taken as a whole do not comply with generally accepted accounting principles. *See* Audit, Audit opinion. *Compare* Qualified audit opinion; Unqualified audit opinion.

AICPA: *See* American Institute of Certified Public Accountants.

American Institute of Certified Public Accountants (AICPA): The professional organization for certified public accountants, the accountants who perform audits.

Ames, Gary Adna: The person to sue for any libelous material in this book. *See Preface to the Second Edition.* Also, the co-author of the first edition of this book.

Amortization: The systematic allocation of the cost of a long-lived, intangible asset as an expense over more than one accounting period, typically the expected life of the asset. *Compare* Depreciation, Depletion.

Annuity: A payment of a fixed amount per period for a specified number of periods.

APB: *See* Accounting Principles Board.

ASB: *See* Auditing Standards Board.

ASR: *See* Accounting Series Releases.

Assets: Tangible and intangible economic resources owned by a business or individual.

Auditing Standards Board (ASB): The committee of the American Institute of Certified Public Accountants responsible for the standards for auditing non-public companies.

Audit inquiry letter: A letter sent to a company's outside lawyers asking them to provide information to the company's auditor about contingent liabilities.

Audit opinion: The report issued by an independent auditor that accompanies a company's financial statements. *See also* Auditor.

Auditor: An independent, outside accountant who issues an opinion on a company's financial statements. *Compare* Internal auditor.

Average cost method: A method of valuing ending inventory based on the average cost of all inventory in stock.

Average fixed cost: The sum of all fixed costs, divided by the number of units produced. *See also* Total cost, Average total cost, Average variable cost, Marginal cost.

Average total cost: The total cost of a given amount of production divided by the number of units produced; the average cost per unit. *See also* Total cost, Average fixed cost, Average variable cost, Marginal cost.

Average variable cost: The sum of all variable costs, divided by the number of units produced. *See also* Total cost, Average total cost, Average fixed cost, Marginal cost.

Balance sheet insolvency: A type of insolvency that exists when the total dollar amount of a company's liabilities exceeds the total dollar amount of the company's assets — in other words, when the total of the equity accounts is negative. *Compare* Cash flow insolvency.

Balance Sheet: An accounting statement that lists assets, liabilities, and equity at a particular point in time.

Basis: The original cost of an asset.

Beginning inventory: The inventory shown on the company's balance sheet at the beginning of an accounting period (equal to ending inventory at the end of the previous period).

Book value: The net value of an asset on a company's balance sheet after subtracting accumulated depreciation. *See* Accumulated depreciation.

Bookkeeping: The system of keeping accounting records, including the accounting journal, accounts for each separate type of asset, liability, or equity, and the financial statements.

Bradford, C. Steven: The author of this book and the father of accounting. Would you believe the uncle? The baby sister?

Capital expenditure: A payment for an asset that will provide benefits over more than one accounting period.

Capital stock: One of the corporate capital accounts. Represents the par value of stock sold by the corporation. Called "stated capital" in some legal sources.

Capital surplus: *See* Additional paid-in capital.

Cash basis of accounting: A method of accounting that recognizes revenues and expenses when a company pays or receives cash. *Compare* Accrual basis of accounting.

Cash flow insolvency: A type of insolvency that exists when a company has insufficient cash to pay its obligations as they become due. *Compare* Balance sheet insolvency.

Cash flow: The movement of cash into and out of a business. *See also* Net cash flow.

Certified public accountant: A licensed accountant who audits financial statements. *See also* Auditor, Audit opinion.

Clean audit opinion: *See* Unqualified audit opinion.

Committee on Accounting Procedure (CAP):   A committee of the AICPA that was one of the FASB's predecessors. It published statements on accounting principles from 1938 to 1959.

Compound interest: Interest paid on both principal and past interest.

Conservatism, principle of: An accounting principle that emphasizes a relatively pessimistic accounting presentation.

Consolidated financial statements: Financial statements that combine the financial results of two or more companies as if they were a single company.

Contingency: A future loss or gain that may or may not occur.

Cost accounting: The collection and interpretation of information about costs.

Cost of goods sold: The expense representing the cost of inventory sold during an accounting period. Cost of goods sold = Beginning inventory + Inventory manufactured or purchased − Ending inventory.

Cost of law school: ∞.

CPA: *See* Certified public accountant.

Credit: A right-hand entry to an accounting record. Also, something your spouse or significant other never gives you.

Debit: A left-hand entry to an accounting record.

Declining-balance method of depreciation: A method of accelerated depreciation in which the percentage of the asset's cost depreciated is some multiple of the straight-line rate. For example, the double-declining-balance method uses twice the straight-line rate and the 150%-declining-balance method uses 1.5 times the straight-line rate. *Compare* Straight-line method of depreciation. *See* Depreciation.

Deferral: Recognizing revenues or expenses in an accounting period later than the period in which the company receives (in the case of revenues) or pays (in the case of expenses) cash or other property. *Compare* Accrual.

Depletion: The systematic allocation of the cost of a natural resource as an expense over more than one accounting period. *Compare* Depreciation, Amortization.

Depreciable cost: The cost of an asset that is to be allocated over multiple accounting periods through depreciation. The depreciable cost does not usually include the asset's salvage value. *See* Depreciation, Salvage value.

Depreciation: The systematic allocation of the cost of an asset as an expense over more than one accounting period, typically the expected life of the asset. When the asset is a natural resource, this allocation is known as depletion. When the asset is an intangible, this allocation is known as amortization. *Compare* Amortization, Depletion.

Direct method of calculating cash flow: A method of calculating cash flow from operations that considers the amount of cash paid or received in connection with each account. *Compare* Indirect method of calculating cash flow.

Discount rate: The interest rate that is used to compute present value — essentially, the return a person could earn on the money if the person had it now.

Double-declining-balance method of depreciation: *See* Declining-balance method of depreciation.

Double-entry bookkeeping: An accounting system in which every transaction produces equal and offsetting entries to a person's accounting records (debits and credits). Debit and credit entries always balance.

Earned surplus: *See* Retained earnings.

Ending inventory: The inventory shown on the company's balance sheet at the end of an accounting period. *Compare* Beginning inventory.

Equity: A section of the balance sheet. The difference between total assets and total liabilities. *See also* Net worth.

Expected present value: A combination of expected value and present value. The present value of an uncertain future outcome, with each possible outcome weighted by its probability. *See* Expected value, Present value.

Expected value: The average value of an uncertain outcome, with each possible outcome weighted by its probability.

Expenses: The costs of the things of value that a business expends in producing revenues.

FASAB: *See* Federal Accounting Standards Advisory Board.

FASB: *See* Financial Accounting Standards Board.

FASB Interpretations: Releases formerly issued by the FASB which explained or clarified existing accounting standards. *See also* Financial Accounting Standards Board (FASB), Accounting Standards Codification.

Federal Accounting Standards Advisory Board (FASAB):   The organization responsible for establishing generally accepted accounting principles for federal government agencies. *Compare* Governmental Accounting Standards Board.

FIFO: *See* First-in, first-out.

Financial Accounting Standards Board (FASB):   A private, independent board designated by the SEC as the standard setter for generally accepted accounting principles in the United States. *See also* International Accounting Standards Board.

Financial Reporting Releases (FRRs):   The most important official statements by the SEC of accounting policies and standards. *See also* Accounting Series Releases (ASRs).

Financing activities: A section of the Statement of Cash Flows. The transactions associated with a business's liabilities and equity accounts — borrowing money and repaying those loans; receiving money from and paying out money to investors. *Compare* Investing activities, Operating activities.

Finished goods: Inventory that a company has manufactured, after the manufacturing process is complete. Included in Inventory on the balance sheet. *Compare* Raw materials, Work in process. *See also* Inventory.

First-in, first-out (FIFO):   A method of valuing ending inventory that assumes the first units of inventory purchased or manufactured by the seller were the first units sold. *Compare* Average cost method, Last-in, first-out.

Fixed costs: Costs that, at least over some range of activity, do not vary with the amount of the activity. *Compare* Variable costs.

FRRs: *See* Financial Reporting Releases.

Fundamental accounting equation: Assets = Liabilities + Equity. This equation is the basis of the balance sheet, which lists assets in one section and liabilities and equity in the other.

Future value: How much a given dollar amount will grow to after a specified period of time at a specified rate of interest. *See also* Time value of money, Present value.

GAAP: *See* Generally accepted accounting principles.

GAAS: *See* Generally accepted auditing standards.

GASB: *See* Governmental Accounting Standards Board.

Generally accepted accounting principles (GAAP): The principles to which financial statements are expected to conform.

Generally accepted auditing standards (GAAS): The standards pursuant to which audits must be conducted.

Governmental Accounting Standards Board (GASB): A private organization responsible for establishing generally accepted accounting principles for state and local governments. *Compare* Federal Accounting Standards Advisory Board.

Handbook of Accounting Standards and Other Pronouncements: A compilation of governmental accounting standards published by the Federal Accounting Standards Advisory Board. *See* Federal Accounting Standards Advisory Board.

Historical cost: The price originally paid to acquire an asset. Most balance sheet values are based on historical cost.

IASB: *See* International Accounting Standards Board.

IFRS: *See* International Financial Reporting Standards.

Income statement: An accounting statement that shows the revenues, expenses, and net income of a business or individual over a specified period of time.

Indirect method of calculating cash flow: A method of calculating cash flow that starts with net income, removes all non-cash items that affect net income, and adds back in all cash items that do not affect net income.

Insolvency: A state of financial difficulty. The term has at least two distinct meanings, balance sheet insolvency and cash flow insolvency. *See* Balance sheet insolvency, Cash flow insolvency.

Internal accounting controls: The accounting system and procedures a company uses to maintain the integrity of its accounting records and to detect financial wrongdoing within the company.

Internal auditor: A company employee who monitors the company's accounting system and reports problems to management. *Compare* Auditor.

Internal controls report: An opinion of a company's auditor reporting on the company's internal controls. *See also* Auditor.

International Accounting Standards Board (IASB): An international body charged with creating internationally accepted accounting principles. *Compare* Financial Accounting Standards Board.

International Financial Reporting Standards (IFRS): The accounting standards developed by the International Accounting Standards Board.

Inventory: Goods held for sale in the regular course of business.

Investing activities: A section of the Statement of Cash Flows. It includes payments to acquire property, plant, and equipment, to make loans, and to make equity investments in other companies. It also includes cash received from selling those assets and investments, and in repayment of the principal on loans made to others. *Compare* Financing activities, Operating activities.

Journal: A chronological listing of a company's financial transactions, with equal debits and credits for each transaction.

Last-in, first-out (LIFO):   A method of valuing ending inventory that assumes the last units of inventory purchased or manufactured by the seller were the first units sold. *Compare* Average cost method, First-in, first-out.

Ledger: The record containing the balances in each bookkeeping account.

Liabilities: Debts or other debt-like obligations owed by a business or individual.

LIFO: *See* Last-in, first-out.

Lower-of-cost-or-market rule: An accounting rule that sometimes requires the value of inventory on the balance sheet to be reduced below its historical cost, with the amount of the write-down treated as an expense.

Management's Discussion and Analysis (MD&A):   A section the SEC requires to be included in the annual reports of public companies that, among other things, includes a narrative discussion of accounting-related issues.

Marginal cost: The additional cost of producing one additional unit after the units before it have already been produced. *See also* Average cost, Average fixed cost, Average variable cost.

Matching principle: The rule that expenses should be recognized when the revenue they helped produce is recognized. *See also* Revenue recognition principle.

MD&A: *See* Management's Discussion and Analysis.

Members' equity: The name of the equity section of a limited liability company, so-called because the equity investors in a limited liability company are known as members.

Net cash flow: The difference between the cash coming into a business and the cash going out of a business.

Net income (or net loss):   Revenues - expenses, for a specified period of time. Net income is the "bottom line" of the income statement — the profit or loss of the business.

Net worth: The name for equity on an individual's balance sheet. The difference between the amount of total assets and the amount of total liabilities. *See also* Equity.

No-par stock: Stock without a par value. *See also* Par value.

Notes to the financial statements: A section at the end of a company's financial statements that contains important disclosures and other information about the company's accounting.

Operating activities: A section of the Statement of Cash Flows. The transactions associated with a business's sales of goods and services in the ordinary course of business. This section also includes interest received on loans the company makes to others and dividends received from stock in other companies. *Compare* Financing activities, Investing activities.

Paid-in capital in excess of par value: *See* Additional paid-in capital.

Paid-in capital in excess of stated value: Another name for the Additional paid-in capital account when the corporation's stock has no par value. *See also* Additional paid-in capital.

Par value: An arbitrary amount designated by a corporation for some classes of stock. Not all stock has a par value. *See also* Capital stock, Additional paid-in capital.

Partners' equity: The name of the equity section on the balance sheet of a partnership, so-called because the equity investors in a partnership are known as partners.

Payable: A type of liability account that represents a company's obligation to pay. *Compare* Receivable.

PCAOB: *See* Public Company Accounting Oversight Board.

Periodic inventory method: A method of tracking inventory that adjusts the inventory account and the cost of goods sold at the end of each period. *Compare* Perpetual inventory method.

Perpetual inventory method: A method of tracking inventory that adjusts the inventory account and the cost of goods sold as each item is sold. *Compare* Periodic inventory method.

Placzek, Sandy: The woman who was crazy enough to marry the author. *See* the *Dedication* to this book.

Present value: The current value of a payment to be made at some point in the future, given a specified interest rate, known as the discount rate. *See also* Time value of money, Future value, Discount rate.

Profit and loss statement: Another name for the income statement. *See* Income Statement.

Public Company Accounting Oversight Board (PCAOB):   A quasi-public, quasi-private regulator of public company auditing principles and auditors.

Qualified audit opinion: An audit opinion issued when the auditor finds a problem with the company's financial statements that does not prevent the financial statements on the whole from fairly presenting the company's financial position. *See* Auditor, Audit opinion. *Compare* Unqualified audit opinion, Adverse audit opinion.

Raw materials: Assets that will be used to manufacture a company's inventory. Included in Inventory on the balance sheet. *Compare* Work in process, Finished goods. *See also* Inventory.

Receivable: A type of asset account that represents a company's right to receive a payment. *Compare* Payable.

Regulation S-X: The SEC's principal accounting regulation.

Replacement cost: A value used in applying the lower-of-cost-or-market rule. What it would cost the company at today's prices to purchase or produce its inventory. *See also* Lower-of-cost-or-market rule.

Reserve account: An account in the equity section of the balance sheet that reflects a possible future contingency that has not been recognized.

Residual value: *See* Salvage value.

Retained earnings: One of the corporate equity accounts. The account to which income and losses are posted. Known in some legal sources as "Earned surplus."

Revenue recognition principle: The rule that revenues should be recognized when the seller substantially completes the earning process.

Revenues: The things of value that a person or business receives from selling goods or performing services.

Risk: The variation among possible outcomes when the exact outcome is uncertain.

Salvage value: The value of an asset at the end of its useful life to the company. The salvage value of an asset is not usually allocated as an expense through depreciation. *See* Depreciation, Depreciable cost.

SEC: *See* Securities and Exchange Commission.

Securities and Exchange Commission (SEC): A U.S. government agency responsible for administering the federal securities laws. It is the primary government regulator of accounting.

Sensitivity analysis: Calculating estimates such as present value or expected value using different plausible payment amounts, discount rates, or probabilities, to see how sensitive the estimate is to changed assumptions.

SFAS: *See* Statement of Financial Accounting Standards.

Shareholders' equity: The name of the equity section on the balance sheet of a corporation, so-called because the equity investors in a corporation are known as shareholders. Also known as Stockholder's equity.

Specific identification: A method of calculating ending inventory and the cost of goods sold that tracks each individual unit of inventory and its cost.

Staff Accounting Bulletins: Statements of accounting interpretations and practices issued by the staff of the SEC. *See also* Securities and Exchange Commission.

Stated capital: *See* Capital stock.

Statement of capital changes: *See* Statement of stockholders' equity.

Statement of cash flows: An accounting statement that tracks a person's cash flow for a specified period of time.

Statement of Financial Accounting Standards (SFAS): A former publication of the FASB, used to establish new accounting standards or principles. *See also* Financial Accounting Standards Board (FASB).

Statement of Governmental Accounting Standards: The most authoritative pronouncement of the Governmental Accounting Standards Board. *See* Governmental Accounting Standards Board.

Statement of Policy Regarding Lawyers' Responses to Auditors' Requests for Information: A statement issued by the American Bar Association governing how lawyers should respond to audit inquiries. *See* Audit inquiry letter.

Statement of stockholders' equity: An accounting statement that explains changes in the equity accounts over a specified period. Also called "Statement of Capital Changes."

Stockholders' equity: *See* Shareholders' equity.

Straight-line depreciation: A method of calculating depreciation expense. The cost of the asset, less its salvage value, is allocated as an expense equally over its useful life. *See* Depreciation.

Sum-of-the-years'-digits method: A method of accelerated depreciation. The depreciation rate for any year is a fraction. The numerator of the fraction is the number of years of useful life remaining (including the current year); the denominator is the sum of the years of useful life. *See also* Depreciation, Accelerated depreciation.

T-account: A method of keeping a running total of debits and credits to an account. Debits appear on the left-hand side of the T and credits appear on the right-hand side of the T.

Time value of money: The idea that money received now is worth more than money received in the future because of the possibility of using or investing the money between now and the future date. *See also* Future value, Present value.

Total cost: The total cost of a given amount of production, including all fixed costs and variable costs. *See also* Fixed costs, Variable costs.

Unit-of-output method: A method of calculating depreciation expense. The useful life of the asset is measured, not in time, but in the number of units the asset is expected to produce. Depreciation expense for a particular period is calculated based on the proportion of those units produced in the period. *See also* Depreciation.

Unqualified audit opinion: An audit opinion that indicates the auditor discovered no material problems with a company's financial statements. Also known as a clean audit opinion. *See* Auditor, Audit opinion. *Compare* Qualified audit opinion, Adverse audit opinion.

Variable costs: Costs that vary with the amount of an activity. *Compare* Fixed costs.

Work in process: Inventory that a company has begun to manufacture, but has not completed. Included in Inventory on the balance sheet. *Compare* Raw materials, Finished goods. *See also* Inventory.

INDEX

[References are to pages.]

A

ACCELERATED DEPRECIATION METHODS
Generally . . . 51–52

ACCOUNTING CONTROLS (See INTERNAL ACCOUNTING CONTROLS)

ACCOUNTING EQUATION
Generally . . . 9

ACCOUNTING JOURNAL ENTRIES 19–23

ACCOUNTING PRINCIPLES, DISCLOSURE OF
(See NOTES TO FINANCIAL STATEMENTS; NOTES TO FINANCIAL STATEMENTS ACCOUNTING CONTROLS)

ACCOUNTING SERIES RELEASES (ASRS)
Generally . . . 76

ACCRUAL (See also CASH BASIS OF ACCOUNTING; DEFERRAL)
Generally . . . 43–45
Accrual basis of accounting . . . 44
Expense, accrued . . . 46–47
Revenues, accrued . . . 46

ACCRUAL BASIS OF ACCOUNTING (See also ACCRUAL; CASH BASIS OF ACCOUNTING; DEFERRAL)
Generally . . . 44

ACCRUED EXPENSE, REPORTING OF
Generally . . . 46–47

ACCRUED REVENUES, REPORTING OF
Generally . . . 46

AMORTIZATION OF INTANGIBLES
Generally . . . 53; 100

ASSETS (See also BALANCE SHEET; LIABILITIES)
Generally . . . 7–9

AUDITING
Audit opinions (See AUDIT OPINIONS)
Auditors (See AUDITORS)
Audit reports (See AUDIT OPINIONS)

AUDIT INQUIRY LETTER
Generally . . . 87–89
Consent of client . . . 87–88
Statement of Policy Regarding Lawyers' Responses to Auditors' Requests for Information . . . 87

AUDIT OPINIONS
Generally . . . 83–85
Clean . . . 84
Qualified . . . 84

AUDITORS (See also CERTIFIED PUBLIC ACCOUNTANT (CPA))
Independent auditors defined . . . 83
Internal auditors defined . . . 83
Oversight of . . . 83

AUDIT REPORTS (See AUDIT OPINIONS)

AVERAGE COST METHOD OF INVENTORY EVALUATION
Generally . . . 58

B

BALANCE SHEET (See also DOUBLE-ENTRY BOOKKEEPING; EQUITY; LIABILITIES)
Defined . . . 7–9

BALANCE SHEET INSOLVENCY
Cash flow insolvency distinguished . . . 38–39
Defined . . . 37

BEGINNING INVENTORY
Defined . . . 56

C

CAPITAL, INVESTMENTS AND WITHDRAWALS OF
Generally . . . 29

CAPITAL CHANGES, STATEMENT OF
Generally . . . 34–35

CAPITAL EXPENDITURES, REPORTING OF
Generally . . . 49

CASH BASIS OF ACCOUNTING
Generally . . . 43

CASH FLOW
Generally . . . 65–70
Defined . . . 65
Operating activities, calculating cash flow from . . . 67–70
Sources of . . . 66–67
Statement of cash flows (See CASH FLOWS, STATEMENT OF)

CASH FLOW INSOLVENCY
Balance sheet insolvency distinguished . . . 38–39
Defined . . . 37

CASH FLOWS, STATEMENT OF
Generally . . . 67–70
Defined . . . 67
Direct method . . . 67
Indirect method . . . 67

CERTIFIED PUBLIC ACCOUNTANT (CPA)
Regulation of . . . 83

[References are to pages.]

[References are to pages.]

F

FASAB (See FEDERAL ACCOUNTING STAN-DARDS ADVISORY BOARD (FASAB))

FASB (See FINANCIAL ACCOUNTING STAN-DARDS BOARD (FASB))

FEDERAL ACCOUNTING STANDARDS ADVI-SORY BOARD (FASAB)
Generally . . . 95

FIFO (See FIRST-IN, FIRST-OUT (FIFO) INVEN-TORY METHOD)

FINANCIAL ACCOUNTING STANDARDS BOARD (FASB)
Generally . . . 75–76
FASAB Handbook of Accounting Standards and Other Pronouncements . . . 95
Statements of Financial Accounting Concepts . . . 76
Statements of Financial Accounting Standards (SFAS) . . . 76
Technical Bulletins . . . 76

FINANCIAL REPORTING RELEASES (SEC)
Generally . . . 76

FINANCIAL STATEMENTS
Obligation to prepare, public companies' . . . 73

FINISHED GOODS, INVENTORY OF
Generally . . . 55

FIRST-IN, FIRST-OUT (FIFO) INVENTORY METHOD
Generally . . . 58; 100

FUTURE VALUE
Generally . . . 116–117
Accuracy of . . . 122
Computation of . . . 119–120

G

GAAP (See GENERALLY ACCEPTED ACCOUNT-ING PRINCIPLES (GAAP))

GASB (See GOVERNMENTAL ACCOUNTING STANDARDS BOARD (GASB))

GENERALLY ACCEPTED ACCOUNTING PRIN-CIPLES (GAAP)
Generally . . . 75–78
Defined . . . 75
Financial Accounting Standards Board (FASB) (See FINANCIAL ACCOUNTING STANDARDS BOARD (FASB))
Internal Revenue Service . . . 77
International Accounting Standards Board (IASB) . . . 77
International Financial Reporting Standards (IFRS) . . . 77
Securities and Exchange Commission (SEC) (See Se-curities and Exchange Commission (SEC))

GOVERNMENTAL ACCOUNTING STANDARDS BOARD (GASB)
Generally . . . 95

H

HISTORICAL COST
Defined . . . 8

I

INCOME STATEMENT
Defined . . . 11
Sample statement . . . 12–13

INSOLVENCY
Generally . . . 37–39
Balance sheet insolvency
　Cash flow insolvency distinguished . . . 38–39
　Defined . . . 37
Cash flow insolvency
　Balance sheet insolvency distinguished . . . 38–39
　Defined . . . 37
Law students . . . 39

INTANGIBLE ASSETS
Defined . . . 8

INTERNAL ACCOUNTING CONTROLS
Generally . . . 91–94
Foreign Corrupt Practices Act . . . 91
Key concepts of . . . 93–94
Public Company Accounting Oversight Board (PCAOB) standards . . . 92
Sarbanes-Oxley Act of 2002 . . . 91

INTERNAL REVENUE SERVICE (IRS)
Generally . . . 77

INTERNATIONAL ACCOUNTING STANDARDS BOARD (IASB)
Generally . . . 77

INTERNATIONAL FINANCIAL REPORTING STANDARDS (IFRS)
Generally . . . 77

INVENTORY
Generally . . . 55–60
Average-cost method . . . 58
Balance sheet valuation . . . 57
Beginning inventory . . . 56
Cost of goods sold, calculation of . . . 56
Ending inventory . . . 56
Finished goods defined . . . 55
First-in, first-out (FIFO) method . . . 58; 100
Last-in, first-out (LIFO) method . . . 58; 100
Lower-of-cost-or-market rule . . . 57
Periodic method of tracking . . . 56
Perpetual method of tracking . . . 56
Raw materials defined . . . 55
Replacement cost . . . 57
Specific identification method . . . 58

[References are to pages.]